Sir Richard Francis Burton

THE WORLD'S GREAT EXPLORERS

Richard Burton

By Charnan Simon

Consultant: Dr. James Casada, Ph.D.,
Professor of History,
Winthrop College,
Rock Hill, South Carolina

 CHILDRENS PRESS®

CHICAGO

Tent-shaped mausoleum housing Richard Burton's remains at Mortlake, a Catholic cemetery in London

Project Editor: Ann Heinrichs
Designer: Lindaanne Donohoe
Cover Art: Steven Gaston Dobson
Engraver: Liberty Photoengraving

Library of Congress Cataloging-in-Publication Data

Simon, Charnan.
  Richard Burton / by Charnan Simon.
    p.   cm. — (The World's great explorers)
  Includes bibliographical references and index.
  Summary: Follows the life and accomplishments of Richard Burton, African explorer, Islamic scholar, discoverer of Lake Tanganyika, and translator of "The Arabian Nights."
  ISBN 0-516-03062-0
  1. Burton, Richard Francis, Sir, 1821-1890—Juvenile literature. 2. Explorers—Great Britain—Biography—Juvenile literature. [1. Burton, Richard Francis, Sir, 1821-1890. 2. Explorers.] I. Title. II. Series.
G246.B8S56 1991
910'.92—dc20   90-20814
[B]   CIP
[92]   AC

Caricature of Burton, the world traveler, in the May 13, 1882, issue of the London magazine Punch

Table of Contents

Chapter 1
Danger in the Night

The African night was dark and still. A row of tents pitched high on a rocky ridge gleamed ghostly white against the sky. In front of the tents, pack camels shuffled their tethered feet in the sand. Farther back, mules and horses shifted and snorted. Silently circling the camp, the sentries assured themselves that all was well.

Inside the center tent, one man was still awake. Captain Richard Francis Burton, leader of the Somali Expedition, filled one page in his journal, then dipped his pen to begin another. Ignoring the insects buzzing around his lantern, Burton wrote on steadily until his entry was complete.

Burton finally put down his pen. He flexed his cramped fingers and listened for a moment. All was quiet. With a satisfied nod, he put out the lantern and prepared for sleep. Tomorrow would be a busy day.

The Somali Expedition had been a long time in the making. For years Richard Burton had wanted to explore Africa's interior. He had heard the stories brought back by Arab slave traders who traveled deep into the heart of the continent. He had talked to Christian missionaries from Abyssinia and Mombasa. Some of the stories had been incredible. A range of mountains south of the equator, that stayed snow-covered all year round? Huge lakes and fountains in the center of the continent, giving rise to such great rivers as the Nile and the Congo?

Just hearing stories had never been good enough for Richard Burton. He wanted to see and experience Africa for himself. Now, in April 1855, he was about to do just that. From this camp near the Red Sea port town of Berbera, he would travel deep into unknown Somalia. He would go across the Horn of Africa, down the coast to the Indian Ocean island of Zanzibar—and then inland to discover the legendary sources of the great Nile River. With this one trip, Richard Burton would venture straight into the heart of Africa, where no European had dared to go before!

Getting support for his expedition hadn't been easy. Constant warfare among the Somali people made traveling through their country dangerous. Even other Africans thought twice before crossing Somali territory. The British government could well imagine how much worse it would be for foreigners. British officials hesitated to give either money or approval to a trip that could easily prove fatal to the average explorer.

Then, too, there was the question of religion. Queen Victoria's Britain was staunchly Christian. Africa was partly Muslim but largely pagan. In some parts of the world, Christians and non-Christians were learning

Beach scene, Zanzibar

to live together in an uneasy peace. But Africa was still a great unknown. Both rumors and real incidents convinced the British that Africa was a dangerous place for the average Christian.

Richard Burton, however, was neither an average explorer nor an average Christian. Just thirty-four years old, he had already traveled all over India and Arabia. He spoke more than twenty languages, including Arabic, Hindustani, Persian, Turkish, and Somali. He had read more Muslim literature and knew more about Muslim customs than any Westerner alive. While in India, he had even converted to Islam, the Muslims' faith. Then, disguised as a wandering Muslim doctor, he had penetrated the secrets of the Islamic holy cities of Mecca and Medina, traveling routes never before taken by any European.

Burton had already journeyed once through Somalia. He was just back from the most harrowing trip of his life, a journey to the forbidden Muslim city of Harar. Before Burton, no European had even known exactly where Harar was. Legend had it that any Christian entering the city's walls would instantly be put to death. Richard Burton had not only found Harar, he had safely left it after a ten-day stay!

If anyone was suited to explore the heart of the African continent, it was Richard Burton. Still, British officials hesitated to let him go. There was no question that he was a brilliant linguist and an intrepid explorer. But he was also an independent, opinionated, and stubborn man. He had made many enemies in his lifetime. Now, some of those enemies were the very officials from whom he had to beg permission to explore Africa.

Finally, after more than a year of argument and compromise, Burton got his expedition. He enlisted three officers from the British East Indian service to go with him. Lieutenant G. E. Herne was a surveyor, photographer, and skilled mechanic. Lieutenant William Stroyan was also a surveyor, as well as a skilled artist. And Lieutenant John Hanning Speke was a surveyor, mapmaker, and expert big-game hunter.

Besides the four British officers, the expedition consisted of forty-two Egyptian, Nubian, Arab, and Somali guards and servants. Rounding out the expedition were some fifty-six pack camels and a score of mules and horses. Early in April 1855, Richard Burton's Somali Expedition was finally gathered together in the Red Sea port of Berbera.

It was the end of a busy time in Berbera. The annual fair was winding down after five long months.

Throughout the fair season, Arab caravans from Africa's interior came to sell the slaves, cattle, coffee, ivory, ostrich feathers, rhinoceros horns, and fine, scented gums they had collected. In exchange, the traders bartered with visiting merchants from India and Arabia for the cotton cloth, beads, dates, and rice they would need for their return trips.

All day, and often well into the night, Berbera rang with the voices of buyers and sellers. Long lines of pack camels paced the yellow shores of the harbor. Dusty lanes were crowded with mat stalls housing the three thousand buyers, sellers, and slaves that had flooded Berbera since November.

Then, on April 9, the first of the monsoon rains fell. It was time for the caravans to begin their long trek back into Central Africa. Throughout the town, mats were stripped from their frameworks of sticks and poles, camels were loaded, and thousands of travelers lined the roads. By the next morning, Berbera was virtually deserted.

Impatiently, Richard Burton watched Berbera empty of people. He and his men had hoped to be leaving with one of the caravans. Despite his confident words to his superiors, Burton knew full well how dangerous his journey through Somalia would be. He also knew that there was safety in numbers. Traveling with an Arab caravan would offer the most safety of all.

Unfortunately, Burton would not have this advantage. The mid-April mail boat from Europe had not yet arrived in Berbera's harbor. Until it did, the Somali Expedition could not get away, for the boat was carrying valuable surveying instruments and other necessities for the expedition.

An Arab caravan at rest

So Richard Burton and his men waited. From their camp they could see both the harbor and the town. With the caravan gone, they knew they were in danger of attack by hostile Somalis. Luckily, the British schooner *Mahi* was anchored just offshore. Should trouble arise, the *Mahi* could offer support and protection.

The first hint of trouble came when the *Mahi* was called out of port, leaving Burton and his men without protection. Still, Burton was not overly concerned. As he would later write, "Briefly, we saw no grounds of apprehension. During thirty years, not an Englishman of the many that had visited it had been molested at Berbera."

Arab dhows at sea

About noon on April 18, a small Arab ship entered the Berbera harbor. On board were a dozen Somalis interested in joining Burton's expedition. Burton agreed to take them along. Then, in what would prove to be a lucky move, he treated the ship's captain and crew to dinner. Instead of leaving Berbera that evening, the ship remained in the harbor throughout the night.

Around sunset on that same night, three strange horsemen came galloping into Burton's camp. Startled, his guards fired three warning shots into the air. Burton hurried from his tent to see what was the matter. Ordering his men to hold their fire, he began to question the strangers closely.

Burton suspected that the three horsemen were Somali scouts planning a raid on the camp. After careful questioning, he was convinced of their innocence, and he let them go. It was to prove a fateful and tragic decision.

Burton's camp prepared for night. The animals were secured, sentries were posted, and the men settled into their tents. Burton and Herne shared a large tent called a Rowtie, while Speke and Stroyan had smaller tents on either side. When all was quiet, Richard Burton finished writing up the day's report in his journal, put out his lantern, and fell peacefully to sleep.

He wasn't to sleep for long. Sometime between two and three in the morning, cries of alarm from the camp guards jolted him awake. The camp was under attack!

Leaping from his bed, Burton heard "a rush of men like a stormy wind." Quickly, he snapped out an order for Lieutenant Herne to scout out what was happening. Then, snatching up his saber, he went to rouse Speke and Stroyan.

Herne seized his Colt revolver and made a quick survey of the camp. Most of the guards had fled in a panic, and the few remaining were overwhelmed by over 350 attacking Somalis. Calling to the guards to follow, Herne turned back to his tent, firing at his attackers as he went.

In the Rowtie, Herne found Burton mounting a desperate defense. Speke, who at first thought the shots were a false alarm, soon realized the attack was real and joined his comrades. Stroyan was nowhere to be seen; after Burton woke him, he became separated from his companions and was never again seen alive.

Guarding the entrance to the Rowtie, Burton, Speke, and Herne fought on. Speke and Herne had a pair of pistols between them, but Burton was armed only with his saber. Dodging clubs, spears, and daggers, the three fought with the desperation of doomed men.

It was a terrifying battle. The enemy swarmed like hornets, and their war cries filled the night. When Herne's ammunition ran out, he threw down his gun and snatched up a spear tied to the tent pole. Turning, he caught sight of an enemy Somali breaking into the rear of the tent. He shouted out a warning to Burton and Speke, who were still fighting just inside the tent's entrance.

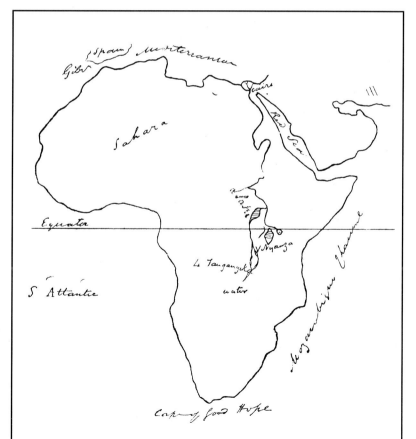

Burton's sketched map of Africa

All three men recognized what was happening. Their Somali attackers were trying to cut the tent ropes and entangle them in the collapsing folds. Thus trapped, the three explorers would be helpless targets for the deadly stabs of enemy spears.

There was only one thing to do. If the three could somehow make their way down the ridge to the sea, they could seek refuge from the friendly Arab ship lying in harbor. It was a slight chance at best—but the only chance they had. Grimly, Burton began hacking his way through the Somalis crouching at the tent entrance. When he saw Speke hesitate, he called out sharply, "Don't step back or they'll think we are retreating!" Stung by what he felt was an attack on his courage, Speke leaped forward into the fray.

Burton was just past the mob when he thought he saw Stroyan's body lying motionless in the sand before him. Slashing and cutting, he moved toward the spot. As he did so, he was hampered by one of his own Somali guards, who, trying to guide Burton to safety, kept getting in the way of Burton's blade.

Not recognizing that the man hanging onto his arm was an ally, Burton turned angrily to cut him down. The guard cried out in alarm, Burton hesitated, and at that moment an enemy Somali stepped forward and hurled his javelin straight through Burton's cheek and jaw.

Reeling from pain, Burton allowed himself to be led to safety by his Somali guard. Another guard appeared, and Burton sent him to find the Arab ship and tell its captain about the attack. Then Burton turned back toward camp, searching desperately for his companions. All night he wandered, sometimes passing out from pain, then rising to continue the search. When day broke, he dragged himself to the harbor and was taken aboard by friendly hands.

Even then Burton couldn't relax. Ignoring his own injuries, he persuaded the ship's crew to arm themselves and go back in search of Speke, Herne, and Stroyan. Only after the rescue party set out did he allow a crewman to wrench the javelin from his jaw and stop the rush of blood flowing from his cheek.

Herne, meanwhile, had fared slightly better than Burton. He, too, fought his way out of the camp, suffering several stiff blows from enemy war clubs. Like Burton, he managed to make his way to the harbor and was taken aboard the Arab ship.

Speke's escape was far more amazing. His revolver failed to fire as he pushed away from the tent, and he was soon clubbed to the ground. With his hands tied behind him, he lay captive throughout the night, watching his Somali captors perform a victory dance around him. Warriors taunted him with their spears, but he escaped serious injury until morning.

Then, just as day broke, yet another Somali warrior approached, brandishing his spear. Speke, who had by now freed his hands, lunged for the spear just as it was leveled at his heart. He managed to turn aside the deadly point but lost his hold when the Somali delivered a crushing club blow to Speke's arm.

The next few moments were a nightmare. The Somali repeatedly stabbed Speke in his hands, arms, shoulders, and both thighs. At last the desperate Speke, "smelling death," as he later put it, leapt to his feet and rushed past his astonished attacker toward the sea. Dodging javelins thrown at his back, he managed to run, walk, and crawl toward the harbor, where he was finally rescued by the ship's search party.

Speke's escape from the Somali

With Burton, Herne, and Speke safe on board, the ship's captain armed his men for a final survey of the expedition's campsite. The Somali attackers had fled, taking with them whatever supplies they could carry.

Lying in front of the tent he had tried so desperately to defend was William Stroyan, dead of a spear wound through the heart.

"This was the severest affliction that befell us," wrote Burton sorrowfully. "We had lived together like brothers."

Photograph of Burton, showing the scar where a javelin pierced his cheek

Thus, Burton's Somali Expedition ended before it had properly begun. Stroyan's body was laid to rest at sea, and Burton, Speke, and Herne went home to England to recover from their wounds. For the rest of his life, Burton would wear a scar on his cheek as a reminder of the disastrous Somali Expedition.

Yet, within a year and a half, Burton would be back in Africa. The call of the Nile was too strong to be silenced by a single defeat or by one ugly scar. The source of the Nile was hidden somewhere deep inside Africa—and Richard Burton meant to find it!

Chapter 2
"Perfect Devilets"

Richard Francis Burton was anything but an ordinary man, and he led anything but an ordinary childhood. In fact, just about the *only* ordinary thing that happened to Richard was being born.

Born at Torquay in Devonshire, England, on March 19, 1821, the squalling, red-haired baby was baptized in proper British fashion. However, he wasn't to remain for long on British soil. Before Richard was a year old, his father took the family to France to live. Though they returned to England for the births and baptisms of Richard's younger sister and brother, the Burtons were never again to live permanently in England.

Richard's father, Colonel Joseph Burton, was a gentleman and an officer in the British army. He suffered from chronic bronchial asthma and retired from active service soon after Richard was born. Throughout Richard's childhood, his father never worked at any particular job. Instead, he wandered from place to place in Europe, searching for the ideal climate for his delicate lungs.

This perfectly suited young Richard's adventurous nature and active curiosity. Without a regular routine to guide him, he grew to be a wild child, though never a cruel or mean one. As one relative later said, Richard was "mischievous as a monkey . . . but with a gentle side to his nature." Or, as another family member put it, Richard was "one of the most troublesome . . . but most warm-hearted boys that ever breathed."

Richard's boyhood games were innocent enough. Some of his happiest memories were of the years the family lived in the medieval French city of Tours. Here Richard and Edward, with their sister Maria, ate clusters of juicy, purple grapes in the garden, set up their wooden Noah's Ark animals under the box hedges, gathered snail shells and cowslips in the shady lanes, and romped with friendly neighborhood dogs.

Life was not all fun and games, however. Richard began studying Latin at home when he was just three, followed by Greek a year later. When Richard was six, Maria four, and Edward three, they started classes in the village school. Besides Greek and Latin, lessons included drawing, dancing, French, music, and—Richard's favorite—the study of swords and other arms.

It was while they were at school in Tours that the children turned into what Richard would later call "perfect devilets." Their favorite sport was fighting their French classmates, using fists, stones, sticks, and snowballs. Next to fighting they liked to skip school, playing Robinson Crusoe in the woods near their home. In between searching out birds' nests and galloping on horseback, they teased their parents and played tricks on the family's servants. Their favorite toys were pop-guns and spring pistols, tin knives and wooden swords.

For the most part, Richard's parents left their children's upbringing to teachers and servants. When Colonel or Mrs. Burton *did* try to discipline the children, the results were disastrous—and hilarious. As Richard would later write: "Our father and mother had not much idea of managing their children; it was like the old tale of the hen who hatched ducklings. By way of a wholesome and moral lesson of self-command and self-denial, our mother took us past Madame Fisterre's windows [the bakery], and bade us look at all the good things in the window, during which we fixed our ardent affections upon a tray of apple-puffs; then she said, 'Now, my dears, let us go away; it is so good for little children to restrain themselves.' Upon this we three devilets turned flashing eyes and burning cheeks upon our moralizing mother, broke the windows with our fists, clawed out the tray of apple-puffs, and bolted, leaving poor mother a sadder and a wiser woman, to pay the damages of her lawless brood's proceedings."

By 1830, Richard's adventures in Tours were about to come to an end. France was in an upheaval from the bloody revolution that had hurled King Charles X from his throne. Even worse was the deadly cholera epidemic raging through the land. Ever cautious where health matters were concerned, Colonel Burton decided to move his family back to England.

It was not a happy move for Richard. All his life he had loved France's sunny skies, light-hearted people, and excellent food and drink. By comparison, England seemed cold, dark, and gloomy. Richard found English people surly and English food "coarse and half-cooked." Though it might be his native country, England would never truly be Richard Burton's home.

Fortunately for Richard, his father seemed to feel the same way. At first Colonel Burton was determined to make his sons proper British gentlemen. He recognized that their education in France had been somewhat irregular. Now he was determined to make up for lost time. Colonel Burton decided that Richard and Edward would someday graduate from one of Britain's famous universities, Oxford or Cambridge. To prepare for the university, they would enroll at Eton, Britain's best preparatory school. And to prepare for Eton, the boys would first attend a lesser school managed by the Reverend Charles Delafosse.

This school turned out to be a dreadful mistake. Lessons were taught poorly, by a man Richard described as "no more fit to be a schoolmaster than the Grand Cham of Tartary." The food was poorly prepared, and portions were so skimpy that Richard often went to bed hungry. All he really learned to do was fight. At one point, he had thirty-two affairs of honor to settle in the schoolroom fighting grounds!

Years later, Richard would write of his school experiences: "That part of life, which most boys dwell upon with the greatest pleasure—school and college—was ever a nightmare to us."

Luckily, the nightmare didn't last long. Before the year ended, an attack of measles broke out in the school. In those days, there were no vaccinations to

A typical gloomy, rainy evening in the English countryside

protect children from this dreaded disease. Several students died, and the Burton brothers were quickly removed from classes.

By this time, Colonel Burton, too, had had enough of Britain's dull and gloomy shores. The children were delighted when their father announced that they would be leaving England, as well as the Reverend Delafosse's school. As Richard put it, "We shrieked, we whooped, we danced for joy," when the family moved once more to their beloved France.

Thus the wandering began again. Life wasn't quite the same this time around, however. For one thing, Colonel Burton had hired a tutor and a governess to travel with the family and look after the children's education.

Mr. DuPre, the tutor, and Miss Ruxton, the governess, had their work cut out for them. They learned this during one of their first walks with their young charges, winding through the boulevards of Paris. Now, Richard, Edward, and Maria had visited Paris often, and they knew the city well. But all was new and strange for their teachers. So Richard hatched a plot. At his whistle, the three children ran off in different directions, easily escaping their bewildered tutor and governess. Laughing, the children returned to their hotel and reported that their unfortunate teachers had been run over by a bus. It wasn't until hours later that Mr. DuPre and Miss Ruxton—hot, tired, and angry from wandering all over Paris trying to find their way home—returned to tell the real truth about the afternoon's excursion.

The streets of Paris

The family soon left Paris, as Colonel Burton and his wife continued their search for the perfect climate. The family tried such cities as Orleans, Blois, Lyons, Avignon, and Marseilles in France; and such Italian sites as Leghorn, Pisa, Siena, Rome, Florence, Capua, Sorrento, and Naples. Then it was back to France, and after that back again to Italy.

Wherever the family went, the children's lessons continued. Showing amazing fortitude, Mr. DuPre stayed with the family until Richard turned eighteen. Miss Ruxton, alas, was just the first in a long string of unsuccessful and unloved governesses. Most left after only a few months. Only one earned the children's respect. Miss Morgan was well read and good-natured and, according to Richard, "was the only one who ever spoke to us children as if we were reasonable beings, instead of scolding and threatening. . . . So Miss Morgan could do with the juniors what all the rest of the house completely failed in doing."

With the various governesses and schoolmasters came a wide variety of subjects to study: Greek and Latin, of course, and mathematics, geography, and history. Dancing and drawing were popular with the children, but not nearly so much so as fencing and chess. Edward became quite an accomplished violinist, but Richard ended his music lessons when, in a rage, he broke his violin over his teacher's head. "It was then," Richard wrote later, "my father made the discovery that his eldest son had no talent for music."

What Richard did have was an extraordinary talent for languages. He quickly and easily mastered French, Italian, Greek, Spanish, German, and Portuguese, as well as many local dialects that were not covered in grammar books.

Scene in Siena, Italy

Richard also had a great zest for life. His enormous energy and curiosity led him to learn much about European art, architecture, and archaeology. His passion for people led him to learn even more about the behavior of human beings wherever he went.

This lively nature sometimes led him into trouble. Once he almost suffocated when he insisted on being lowered into a famous Italian cave called the Grotto del Cane. Another time he nearly fell into the smoking crater of Mount Vesuvius. One night he dressed up as an Italian undertaker and went on midnight rounds collecting the stiff, blackened corpses of cholera victims.

Whatever Richard did, Edward was his willing partner. When they didn't feel like studying, they threw

Smoke exuding from Mount Vesuvius near Naples, Italy

their books out the window and went off pistol-shooting or fencing.

It wasn't long before the two had discovered the pleasures of drinking wine, smoking cigars, and writing love poetry to the beautiful daughters of their French and Italian landlords. When their father threatened punishment after one of their escapades, the boys climbed up the rooftop chimneys and refused to come down until all was forgiven.

This wild life couldn't last forever. When Edward wound up in jail after another night's adventure, Colonel Burton had had enough. Once again he packed up his sons and sent them "home" to England. Richard's wandering days were over—for the moment.

As he wandered the streets of Naples, Richard may have seen people making macaroni in the traditional way.

Chapter 3
On to Oxford

Richard Burton's second impression of his native England was no better than his first had been, ten years earlier. While Edward, now just sixteen, was packed off to study with a private tutor, nineteen-year-old Richard went straight to Oxford University.

He did not like what he saw. The countryside looked flat and uninteresting, the rivers seemed like mere ditches, the skies were always grey, and the smell of smoke from the university's many coal fires "was a perpetual abomination."

Richard's introduction to his classmates was just as grim. All summer Richard had worked hard at growing a splendid mustache that was the envy of his European friends. But in 1840, men in England were clean-shaven. As Richard passed through the college gates for the first time, a fellow student met him—and laughed in his face.

Stung, Richard challenged the student to a duel. After all, his personal honor had been insulted. In France or Italy, fighting a duel with pistol or sword would have been the only solution. But this was England. As Richard was to learn, over and over, things were different in England. The boy was astonished at Richard's challenge. Explanations were offered, apologies were exchanged, and the boys parted—one snickering, one sorrowful.

This was just the first of many disappointments for Richard at Oxford. There were his studies, for example. Oxford had been founded as a school for religious studies. Though it was no longer run by the church, the university's religious ties were still very strong. Colonel Burton wanted Richard to graduate from Oxford as a clergyman. This called for a course of study in which Richard had absolutely no interest.

Then, too, though Richard could speak French, Portuguese, Italian, Spanish, Greek, and even Latin like a native, he had not had the "classical" education his teachers expected. They were horrified when he spoke Latin like a Roman and Greek like an Athenian. In those days, educated Englishmen spoke *all* languages with a "proper" British accent!

Richard didn't fit in with his fellow students, either. Most of them had led very similar lives. They came from conventional, thoroughly British families. Many had known each other for years, going to the same preparatory schools, and then to Eton, before arriving at Oxford. They wore the same kinds of clothes, sported the same haircuts, knew the same people, and laughed at the same jokes. Richard, with his fencing and shooting, his European manners, and his familiarity with European languages and customs, just didn't

Seal of Oxford University, 1300

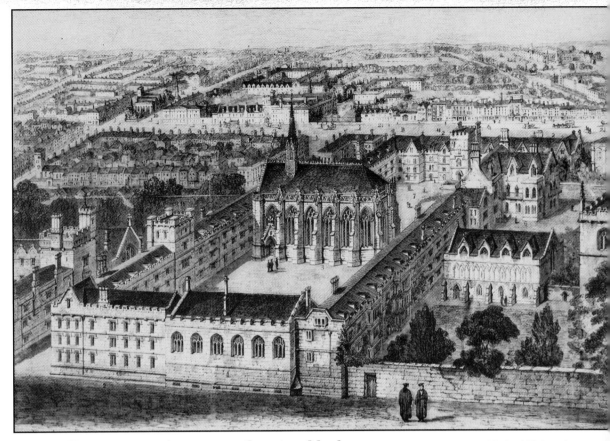

The campus of Oxford University

belong. He was an exotic, a parrot thrust suddenly among the pigeons.

Still, life at Oxford was not a total waste. Richard sought out the few professors who could teach him what he wanted to learn. On his own he began studying Arabic, aided by a sympathetic Spaniard named Don Pascual de Gayangos.

Frustrated by the Oxford method of learning languages, Richard devised his own system. First he got a simple grammar and vocabulary book. In it he marked the most important words and word forms. He then memorized these words by carrying the book around in his pocket and repeating them in spare moments. The key, Richard found, was to study in short, quick bursts. "I never worked more than a quarter of an hour at a time, for after that the brain lost its freshness."

After learning some three hundred words (which Richard claimed was easily done in a week), he started reading a simple story book. He always read aloud to practice the sounds of the words. When he came across new words, he underlined them so he could come back and repeat them. Finally, Richard would study a more complicated grammar book and then try a more difficult reading book, "one whose subject most interested me." Within two months, Richard claimed he could learn any language well enough to read and converse with ease!

Richard made friends at Oxford, too, and took part in the usual college pranks. (He found these pranks rather tame, though, after his and Edward's adventures in Europe!) His favorite place was the fencing room. Here he spent many happy hours sharpening his skill with the sword and making friends that would last him a lifetime.

But for all this, Richard was never happy at Oxford. He disliked the school—and disliked even more the thought of becoming a clergyman. Time and again he begged his father to let him leave Oxford and join the army instead of the clergy, but his father refused to budge.

Finally Richard decided to take matters into his own hands. If his father wouldn't let him leave Oxford honorably, he would leave dishonorably. In fact, he would get himself thrown out of the university! Richard spent most of his second year at Oxford plotting pranks that he thought were bound to get him suspended. His plan was to be "rusticated," or temporarily suspended for not following the rules. Instead, he found himself expelled—permanently suspended for "ungentlemanly conduct." It was quite a blow to a

Oxford students rowing on the Thames River

young man who prided himself on his honor, and he never really forgave Oxford for it.

What was Richard's actual "crime"? He, along with a few friends, attended a forbidden horse race. That in itself was not so serious a crime. But while his friends meekly accepted their punishment, Richard argued that the race should never have been forbidden to students in the first place.

It was the wrong approach to take. The Oxford authorities didn't like Richard's argument, they didn't like his attitude, and they didn't like his arrogance. Without further ado, Richard Burton was expelled from Oxford in the spring of 1842.

Chapter 4
Mirza Abdullah
and the Sind

Now that Richard was out of Oxford, what was to be done with him? For years he had begged his father to let him join the army. Any army would do—the regular British army, the Swiss Guards at Naples, even the French Foreign Legion. Now, finally, Colonel Burton was resigned to the fact that neither of his sons would ever be clergymen. Giving in at last, the colonel allowed both Edward and Richard to accept commissions in the army.

It was an exciting time for England and for young, adventure-loving Englishmen. Queen Victoria had been crowned just four years earlier, in 1838. This marked the beginning of a sixty-three-year reign that would take Great Britain to the height of its national powers. For now, the British Empire was just beginning to extend its reign to colonies all over the world.

Queen Victoria in her coronation robes

In the Far East, there were the riches of China. The Treaty of Nanking in 1842 ended the three-year Opium War between Britain and China. This treaty left the important and profitable island of Hong Kong under British rule.

In the South Pacific, Australia and New Zealand were exciting frontiers for young men anxious to make names for themselves. Even more enticing, however, were Britain's land holdings in India. The rich subcontinent of India would prove to be the cornerstone of the British Empire.

For now, Britain needed soldiers in India, both to guard Britain's trade interests and to subdue any native threats to British rule. There were two separate branches of English armed forces in India. One was the official British army—the Queen's service. The other fell under the control of the Honorable East India Company.

It was to the Honorable East India Company that Richard Burton turned when he left Oxford. This company had been founded in 1600—seven years before the founding of the English settlement at Jamestown, Virginia. Its founders were a group of traders who wanted to profit from India's ivory, silks, and spices. As the company's traders went deeper and deeper into India, the directors began hiring guards to protect them. The ranks of these guards gradually increased to become an entire army.

The role of the East India Company's army was simple. The directors decided where they wanted to expand their trade, then they sent in the army to sign trade agreements with local princes. Once that was accomplished, the army pulled out. Only a small garrison of mixed British and Indian troops remained to

Original coat of arms of the British East India Company

Native Indian officers and soldiers in the East India Company's service

collect taxes and enforce British rule. Though the East India Company was not a government force, the British government had fully supported its actions for over 250 years.

While Richard Burton was growing up in Europe and being miserable at Oxford, the East India Company was looking at lands to the north and west of India—the Sind, the Punjab, and Afghanistan. Englishmen did not question their country's right to conquer and control these faraway lands. After all, they reasoned, Britons were white, educated, and civilized. Naturally, they would be better at ruling than the "uncivilized" and dark-skinned native Indians. And just as naturally, Britain should profit from India's trade goods.

Women of India, as depicted by a nineteenth-century artist

Religion was another issue. Queen Victoria's England was Christian, while India's people were mainly Muslim and Hindu. Many Britons felt it was their sacred duty to convert these "heathen" unbelievers to the true faith of Christianity. So, along with the soldiers and traders, British missionaries had carved out a niche in India.

Today, it doesn't seem surprising that India's people would have resented British rule. Certainly, mid-nineteenth-century India was not as advanced as Britain in some ways. It was still primarily an agricultural society, while Britain was in the full swing of the industrial revolution. India's civilization had flourished for thousands of years. Its art, architecture, literature, music, dance, philosophy, and religion were highly sophisticated. However, they were very different from

Mosque in Ahmedabad, northwest India. Ahmedabad district was the site of an anti-British rebellion in 1918. It was also the scene of political activity by Indian nationalist leader Mahatma Gandhi in 1930.

British and European arts, philosophies, and religions. For many people in Victorian England, "different" meant "not as good."

Politically, India was made up of several small states governed by local princes. There was no real central government to oppose the British invasion. While the princes and their royal families led rich, luxurious lives, most Indians were quite poor. They were too busy finding food and shelter to protest the British plunder of their states.

It came as a surprise to everyone when, in January 1842, the people of Afghanistan rose up against the British armies moving into their mountains. Some sixteen thousand British and Indian troops and their followers died as they retreated from the Afghans through bitterly cold mountain passes.

It was this massacre that prompted young Richard Burton to press for service in the Indian army. He eagerly accepted his commission into the 18th Regiment of the Bombay Native Infantry in June 1842. But by the time he had made the four-month sea journey from England to Bombay, India, the Afghan war was over.

Disappointed that he couldn't make a name for himself as a military hero, Richard turned instead to the study of languages. He wrote later: "In India two roads lead to preferment. The direct highway is 'service'—getting a flesh wound, cutting down a few of the enemy, and doing something eccentric, so that your name may creep into a dispatch. The other path, study of the languages, is a rugged and tortuous one; still, you have only to plod steadily along its length, and sooner or later, you must come to a staff appointment."

Photograph of the Borah bazaar in Bombay, India, from a book by Isabel Burton

Richard had begun to study Hindustani before he even landed in India. Within six months, he had learned enough of the language to place first among eleven men in an interpreter's exam. In another four months he qualified—again, by scoring highest on the exam—as an interpreter of yet another native tongue, Gujarati. In the next six years, he was to master ten more languages and dialects—Marathi, Sindhi, Punjabi, Telugu, Pashto, Miltani, Persian, Arabic, Turkish, and Armenian.

India gave Richard a golden opportunity to show off his ease with languages, but it was a disappointment in other ways. He found that British military society in India was as rigid and narrow-minded as university society had been at Oxford. The British officers and their wives looked down on native Indians as inferior. They made no attempt to learn about Indian ways of life. Despite the enormous differences in climate and culture between England and India, they clung stubbornly to their "proper" British habits and rules of conduct.

Richard had no patience for such an attitude. Here was India—vast, mysterious, complex, and swarming with people of all colors, races, languages, and religious beliefs. For a man with Richard's zest for life, India was an open door to adventure.

Richard decided simply to ignore British military society and to plunge straight into the heart of India. He visited the bazaars, collected rare Oriental manuscripts, learned snake charming, and even, so the story goes, muzzled and rode a crocodile. He exchanged his formal army uniform for more comfortable native dress, the loose-fitting cotton shirt and pants that were called "pajamas." He learned to survive blazing suns and

Indian snake charmer

temperatures rising to 120 degrees Fahrenheit (49 degrees Celsius), as well as drenching monsoon rains that fell for months at a time. And wherever he went, whatever he did, he kept meticulous notes about the cultures and beliefs of the people he met.

All this time, Richard was still an officer in the army, and he didn't neglect his military obligations. Britain was at this time trying to add the northwest province of Sind (in today's Pakistan) to its Indian empire. Richard, with his extensive knowledge of Indian languages and culture, was first used as an interpreter. Later he became a field surveyor, working to rebuild the vast Indus River irrigation system.

Somewhere along the line, Richard began to go out on missions for Sir Charles Napier. Sir Charles was the British officer who finally conquered the Sind. His military victories added over 50,000 square miles (129,500 square kilometers) of northern India to Queen Victoria's empire. An eccentric and outspoken Scotsman, he had many enemies in the British army—and many loyal supporters as well. Sir Charles took a special liking to the brilliant, witty, and unconventional Richard Burton. It wasn't long before he was sending the young officer out on missions whose nature has still never been exactly determined.

Sometimes disguised as a native servant, sometimes as a Muslim holy man, sometimes as a half-Arab, half-Iranian merchant named Mirza Abdullah, Richard traveled throughout the wastes and villages of the Sind. Richard later described Mirza Abdullah thus: "With hair falling upon his shoulders, a long beard, face and hands, arms and feet, stained with a thin coat of henna, Mirza Abdullah of Bushire—your humble servant—set out upon many and many a trip."

Sir Charles Napier

44

Burton in one of his disguises

As Mirza Abdullah, Richard visited Muslim mosques, argued theology with Arabic students, and played chess with Persian scholars. Drinking tea and munching dates, he gossiped with village matchmakers, discussed prices and goods with bazaar merchants—even gracefully refused the fathers who offered him their daughters in marriage! As Richard would later write about Mirza Abdullah, "What scenes he saw! What adventures he went through! But who would believe, even if he ventured to detail them?"

Still, Richard did venture to detail a great deal of Mirza Abdullah's trips. Wherever he went, he picked up valuable information for Sir Charles, information that no ordinary British officer could ever procure.

As he traveled, Burton became more and more intrigued with and impressed by the Muslims' faith. In his usual energetic way, he began a thorough study of the Islamic religion. After months of intensive work, he completed all the rituals of prayer (sometimes four thousand repetitions of the same prayer daily!), fasting (at least forty days' worth, based on Moses' fast in the desert), and study to become a convert to Islam. It was quite a feat. "To this I devoted all my time and energy. . . . I conscientiously went through the *chilla*, or quarantine of fasting and other exercises, which, by-the-by, proved rather over-exciting to the brain . . . and I became a Master-Sufi."

Eventually, Burton's travel, work, and study took its toll on his health. Troubled by recurring fevers and

Burton in 1848 in native dress

Ornate sandstone doorway in the ancient city of Multan. The Sikhs of the Punjab, under the great chief Ranjit Singh, took Multan in 1818. Multan came under British rule in 1849.

an annoying eye infection that he called rheumatic ophthalmia, he took a long sick leave.

Burton was back in active service by 1848, just in time for the uprising of native Sikh chieftains against the British in the Punjab region. Anxious to take part in this military campaign, he asked to be appointed interpreter to the army setting out for the Sikh stronghold of Multan.

He did not get the job. Though he was the only interpreter who knew the Multani language, the appointment went to an officer far less qualified than he. It was a severe blow. Richard Burton was a brilliant linguist and an acknowledged expert on Indian life and culture. He was intelligent, energetic, and courageous. But he was also arrogant, independent, and opinionated. For all the friends he had in high places, he had at least as many enemies.

There were many reasons for this. Richard Burton was never one to yield to authority. It was well known that he had no patience for army politics. Many of his official reports had been critical of the East India Company and its management of Indian affairs. Naturally, his superiors did not take kindly to this criticism.

Then, too, Burton had always scorned the conventional life of the British soldier in India. His familiarity with native Indian life and culture made him a valuable interpreter and guide. Yet, that very familiarity made his fellow officers suspicious of him. Richard Burton was just too Indian for these officers' comfort.

Finally, there was Richard's endless curiosity about human nature. As he traveled about India, he reported on all that he saw. Birthing practices, initiation rites, wedding and funeral rituals, religious services—if it had to do with people and their customs, Richard found it worthy of notice.

But society in Victorian England was rigidly moral. The taboos of the time would make a modern head spin. Burton had no patience for this "immodest modesty," as he called it. In his interested, matter-of-fact way, he wrote about subjects that would make a proper British gentleman blush and avert his eyes. No custom was too shocking for him to study. To many people, this made Burton a dangerous man. He was both scholarly and enthusiastic—and nothing seemed to embarrass him!

All in all, Richard Burton was simply not a good "company man." The interpreter's job in the Punjab was just one of many honors and promotions that would be lost to him throughout his long and varied

Indian bridal procession

career. Try as he might, Richard never *could* behave as other people thought he should.

Broken in spirit and in health, Richard Burton took a leave of absence from the East India Company and quit India. "This last misfortune broke my heart. I had been seven years in India, working like a horse, volunteering for every bit of service. . . . Sick, sorry, and almost in tears of rage, I bade adieu to my friends and comrades in Scinde. . . . My career in India had been, in my eyes, a failure. . . ."

Chapter 5
Pilgrimage to Mecca and Medina

Feelings of disappointment and failure couldn't keep Richard Burton down for long. After a brief visit to relatives in England, he went to Pisa, Italy, and then Boulogne, France, to live with his mother, sister, and his sister's two young daughters.

Surrounded by four adoring females, Richard soon recovered his health and natural energies. Between 1849 and 1853, he published four books on his experiences in India and another on the art of bayonet fighting. His India books were rich in the sort of detail that made conventional Britons nervous. Though most did not receive good reviews at the time, they have since been recognized as classics in their field. Likewise, his *Complete System of Bayonet Exercise* was at first ignored by the British military, for whom it was intended. Later, however, the army adopted many of Burton's suggestions.

Even as Burton was feverishly writing his books, he was busy planning another adventure. Studying Islam had led him to a fascination with all things Arabic. Now he wanted to see Arabia, the birthplace of Islam, for himself. Specifically, he wanted to visit the Muslim holy cities of Mecca and Medina.

Mecca, located some ten miles (sixteen kilometers) inland from the Red Sea in western Saudi Arabia, is the holiest of Muslim cities. It was there that the prophet Muhammad, founder of Islam, was born. All devout Muslims attempt a pilgrimage, or *hajj*, to Mecca during their lifetimes.

Medina is Islam's second-holiest city. It, too, is located in western Saudi Arabia, but about 100 miles (161 kilometers) inland from the Red Sea. Muhammad's tomb in the Prophet's Mosque there is among the most sacred shrines in the Islamic world.

The sacred sites in Mecca and Medina have always been forbidden to non-Muslims. In 1853, any Westerner discovered visiting the shrines in either city faced the possibility of instant death. But the thought of danger did not stop Richard Burton. "It was always my desire to visit Meccah during the pilgrimage season; written descriptions by hearsay of its rites and ceremonies were common enough in all languages, European as well as native, but none satisfied me, because none seemed practically to know anything about the matter."

So Richard Burton began his preparations. Assuming his old disguise as a wandering mirza, he set sail for Alexandria, Egypt, on April 14, 1853, on the steamer *Bengal*.

In Alexandria he spent some time reviewing the Islamic faith, practicing his prayers, and memorizing

Burton as Shaykh Abdullah, with long hair, darkened skin, and flowing robes

the holy book of Islam, the Koran. He grew his hair long and bathed in walnut stain to darken his skin. He also became a *hakim*, or doctor, and named himself Shaykh Abdullah. As a doctor and dervish, or wandering mystic, he would be welcome anywhere in the Muslim world—so long as no one saw through his disguise!

From Alexandria he traveled three days by steamer to Cairo. "We saw nothing but muddy water, dusty banks, sand, mist, milky sky, glaring sun, breezes like the blasts of a furnace . . . the sun burnt us all day, and the night dews were raw and thick. Our diet was bread and garlic, moistened with muddy water from the canal."

From Cairo, Burton set out on a grueling, 84-mile (135-kilometer) ride across the desert of eastern Egypt. Despite the blazing heat and terrible, sandy solitude, Burton gloried in this desert travel. Exuberant, he wrote, "In such circumstances . . . your fancy and imagination are powerfully aroused, and the wildness and sublimity of the scenes around you, stir up all the energies of your soul . . . and believe me, you will suffer real pain in returning to . . . civilization."

At the city of Suez he embarked on a pilgrim ship, or *sambuk*, crowded with barefoot, bareheaded, dirty, ferocious, and armed pilgrims. After twelve days of torturously slow sailing across the Red Sea, he landed at Yenbo on the Arabian Peninsula. Yenbo was the port city nearest to Medina, or Al-Medinah, as it was then called.

Encampment of Muslim pilgrims in the harbor of Alexandria

Now the real fun began. As long as Burton was near the Red Sea, escape was possible, should anyone see through his disguise. But Medina lay over 100 miles (161 kilometers) inland. Once in the middle of the desert wastes, Richard Burton's skillful impersonation of Shaykh Abdullah was his only hope for survival.

Undaunted, Burton hired camels and servants, put his gear in order, and set out on an eight-day journey across a desert whose wind roared "like the breath of a volcano." A severely infected foot (the result of the poisonous bite of a sea urchin) made walking impossible. Cheerfully, he rode on a litter slung over a camel's hump.

By now Burton had made many Muslim friends. He listened spellbound as they spun endless tales about bedouins, the desert nomads. At night, alone in his tent, he would write all that he had heard and learned during the day. To avoid being caught—note-taking was a dangerous practice that would immediately unveil him as a Westerner—he attached a guide wire to his notebook so he could write in the dark and hid his notes among his personal effects.

The journey continued. Attacks by bedouin bandits were minor irritations. "We lost twelve men, camels, and other beasts of burden; the Bedawi [Bedouin] looted the baggage and ate the camels."

As they neared Medina, the caravan had to cross a ridge of black rock so steep that a flight of steps had been cut into it. The nimble-footed camels climbed these steps with ease and hurried down the lava-strewn slope on the other side. Suddenly, there before them lay the gardens, orchards, and minarets of the holy city.

Burton gave thanks like any weary, grateful pilgrim, then proceeded into the city. For a month he was the honored guest at the home of Shaykh Hamid, one of the many friends he had made along the caravan route. During this month he visited all the holy shrines, as any good Muslim would. Wherever he went, he observed the strictest Muslim laws and rituals to the letter. To be uncovered now would mean certain death. And still, despite all obstacles, he managed to make careful notes on every shrine he visited, every Muslim he spoke to. History, geography, archaeology, anthropology—nothing escaped his notice.

After some six weeks in Medina, Burton was ready to push on to Mecca. Though his host warned him of the dangers, Burton was delighted when told he could join the Darb el Sharki caravan. The Darb el Sharki, or inland route, had never before been taken by any European. Cutting inland across the desert instead of following the easier coastal road, the Darb el Sharki was waterless except for a few heavily guarded wells sunk in the eighth century A.D. Following its torturous route would indeed be a challenge—or, as Richard Burton happily put it, "Here was my chance!"

The first portion of the journey was easy enough. The flat desert lands were interrupted by mud-walled villages and cultivated fields. Ample crops of wheat, barley, corn, and even dates provided fresh food.

Soon enough the landscape changed. "The horizon was a sea or mirage; gigantic sand-columns whirled over the plain; and on both sides of our road were huge piles of bare rock, standing detached upon the surface of sand and clay. . . . It was a desert peopled only with echoes—a place of death for what little there is to die in it. . . ."

The holy city of Medina

The caravan traveled mainly at night through these desert wastes. Carcasses of the horses, donkeys, and camels that had died of heat and exhaustion littered the way. Soldiers guarding the occasional wells charged small fortunes for the brackish, foul-tasting water.

Finally the caravan reached Al-Zaribah. It was here that all travelers underwent *Al-Ihram*, or the assuming of pilgrim garb. Men's heads were shaved, and everyone was bathed, perfumed, and dressed in official pilgrim costume. Proper codes of behavior were reviewed. There was to be no killing of any living thing, "nor should we scratch ourselves, save with the open palm, lest vermin be destroyed, or a hair up-rooted by the nail." And while pilgrims were welcome to seek out shady places, they were forbidden to cover their heads from the blistering sun.

Still more dangers lay ahead. Dust storms blinded the pilgrims, and dark, angry-looking cliffs rose up on either side. In the dreaded Pass of Death were ambushing bandits, whom the pilgrims bravely resisted. Then there was one final steep, rocky pass to climb. Threading dark and narrow passageways, the pilgrims arrived at last in that holiest of holy cities—Mecca!

In what he was later to call "an ecstasy of gratified pride," Burton visited all the sacred shrines. For six days he lived intimately with his Muslim hosts. He drank holy water that caused nausea, diarrhea, and boils. He ate meat from sacrificial lambs. Once he was nearly trampled in a camel stampede; another time he was almost crushed by a crowd of sweating, sobbing pilgrims struggling to kiss a holy shrine. His feet were torn by rocky mountain paths, and his head was blistered raw with sunburn.

Burton's caravan making camp in the desert

Everywhere he went, he asked questions, made observations, and took notes. At great personal risk, he paced and measured and sketched the holy sites of Islam, knowing that, as a Christian, "nothing could preserve him from the ready knives of enraged fanatics if detected."

Then, at last, Burton's adventure was over. He had absorbed enough information and taken enough notes to fill three fat volumes. He had gone where no Westerner had dared go before. In the process, he had learned more about Muslim life than any other European in the world. Certainly, he had risked death more times on this one trip than most travelers do in a lifetime. But for now, his curiosity and love of adventure was satisfied. As he would write somewhat wistfully, "I now began to long to leave Mecca. . . . I had done everything and seen everything. . . ."

A woodcut of Mecca in the 1850s

Chapter 6
Breaking the
Guardian's Spell

After Mecca, Richard Burton sailed up the Red Sea and on to Cairo. Here he rested for several weeks, putting his notes in order and planning what he should do next. News of his pilgrimage had already reached the London press. Had he returned to England, he no doubt would have been hailed a hero and won the fame and honor he longed for.

But Burton's leave from the East India Company was almost up. He was due back in Bombay in March 1854; it was already October 1853. There simply wasn't time for a sea journey to London and back, so Richard sailed to Bombay. He worked feverishly to complete his three-volume *Personal Narrative of a Pilgrimage to Al-Medinah and Meccah*, which was published in 1855-1856. Then he began to lay plans for his next adventure.

This time, Richard Burton's goal was Africa. Specifically, he wanted to reach yet another holy and forbidden Muslim city—the legendary Harar.

The walled city of Harar was located in Somaliland (today's Ethiopia) in East Africa. It was both Somaliland's religious capital and the center of the East African slave trade. Though it was only some 150 miles (241 kilometers) from the coast, no European had ever entered it. Legend had it that the first foreigner to walk through Harar's gate would bring doom to the city. It was little wonder that Harar's rulers viewed strangers with suspicion!

Storming Harar's defenses was a challenge Burton couldn't resist. In his usual disguise as a wandering Muslim—this time distinguished by the title of *hajji*, or one who had visited Mecca—he would go to Harar. "All heretofore who have attempted it were murdered. It was therefore a point of honor with me to utilize my title of Haji by entering the city, visiting the ruler, and returning in safety, after breaking the guardian's spell."

Visiting Harar was only a small part of Burton's grand plan. Besides breaking the "guardian's spell," Burton intended to explore the whole of East Africa. He would begin at the Red Sea port city of Berbera. From there he would swing inland to Harar, then head in a southeasterly direction to the Indian Ocean coast. The initial expedition would end with a thorough study of the island of Zanzibar. Once this was accomplished, Burton thought privately, more ambitious expeditions could be launched. Expeditions to discover the mysterious hidden sources of the Nile River, for example. Or even to open a safe east-west route across Africa, from the Indian Ocean to the Atlantic Ocean.

Island and town of Zanzibar, opposite the East African coast

But first there was Somaliland. Burton knew that the Royal Geographical Society in London had long been interested in this part of Africa. Since 1849, the society had been trying to convince the East India Company to release an officer from active duty to "explore the productive resources of the unknown Somali country in East Africa." With the backing of such an important society, he began to make his preparations.

First, he selected three other officers to accompany him. Lieutenant William Stroyan was an accomplished surveyor and artist. Lieutenant G. E. Herne was also a surveyor, as well as a man "skilful in photography and mechanics." The third man, Assistant Surgeon J. E. Stocks, was a medical doctor, a botanist, and an experienced traveler in primitive areas.

Colonel James Outram, who was a distinguished British army commander in India

Burton, Herne, and Stroyan arrived in the Red Sea port city of Aden in October 1854. Here the expedition ran into trouble. The first blow was news of the unexpected death of Stocks in London. The second was the discovery that the East India Company officials in Aden included several of Burton's old enemies from his India days. One in particular, Colonel James Outram, was violently opposed to Burton's plans. Somaliland was too dangerous to travel through, Outram argued publicly. Privately, he made it known that he didn't think Burton was the man to lead such an expedition anyway.

It wasn't the first time Richard Burton's plans had been thwarted by unsympathetic officials. It wouldn't be the last. With a sigh, Burton set about making compromises.

First, he took on Lieutenant John Hanning Speke as Stocks's replacement. The twenty-seven-year-old Speke had served in the Indian army since he was seventeen. During that time he earned a reputation as a courageous soldier and a passionate big-game hunter. Speke had some experience in surveying and mapmaking, but his main interest in Africa was hunting, not exploring. Even though he lacked Stocks's qualifications, Speke was young, strong, adventurous—and available.

Burton next agreed to alter his grand plan somewhat. Instead of all four men traveling together, they would split up for some preliminary explorations. Herne (and later Stroyan) would go to Berbera to explore the coastal mountains and make notes on the slave trade and local commerce. Speke would explore the Wadi Nogal, a famous valley and stream supposedly rich in gold. He would also buy the horses and camels to use on future expeditions.

John Hanning Speke

An old Arab town in Somalia

    Meanwhile, Burton would make the dangerous journey to Harar. If all went well, the four men would meet in Berbera early in 1855. They could then strike out together on the expedition to Zanzibar.

    Once the plan was settled, Burton began his preparations. First, he undertook a thorough study of the Somali language. Dressed as a pious Arab *hajji*, he spent a month in the Somali town of Zayla, talking, listening, and taking endless notes on Somali customs. With his usual vigor, he threw himself into the role of pious Muslim. He led prayers in the mosque and argued fine points of Islam with the Arabs, Somalis, Persians, and Indians who lived in the town. At night, he regaled his listeners with stories from *The Thousand and One Arabian Nights*. Wherever he went, he was admired for his strength and courage and respected for his vast learning.

Arab caravan traveling through the cool desert at night

By the end of November 1854, Burton was ready to leave for Harar. His caravan consisted of five camels, four mules, five guides, and two women cooks. Once outside of town, the guides abandoned their "town" manners and became thoroughly Somali. They greased their hair, oiled and blackened their spears, and put away the guns Burton had given them. To the Somali, guns were a coward's weapon. Spears, daggers, and war clubs were the weapons chosen by true warriors!

The women cooks, too, were people to be reckoned with. Huge and tireless, they bore their burdens without complaint throughout the roughest terrain. As Burton marveled, "To relieve their greatest fatigue, nothing seems necessary but the 'Jogis': they lie at full length, prone, stand upon each other's backs trampling and kneading with the toes, and rise like giants much refreshed."

Hyena in Serengeti Park, Tanzania (formerly Tanganyika)

Scorpion

So the caravan proceeded. Rising early each day, they marched until the blistering sun became too hot at mid-morning. A nap until late afternoon refreshed everyone, and the march resumed until midnight.

Traveling at night was cooler, but it held its share of dangers. Poisonous snakes and scorpions were harder to spot, as were the ankle-twisting holes of rats, squirrels, and lizards. Hyenas howled and jackals barked, startling the pack animals. Every fifteen minutes or so, the whole caravan would stop to adjust the slipping loads of the camels. It was, as Burton noted, "an operation never failing to elicit a vicious grunt, a curve of the neck, and an attempt to bite."

As they traveled, the caravan passed troops of gazelles and the occasional shy ostrich. Though this was the land of lions, leopards, and elephants, Burton only saw a single lion, a huge one that stealthily tracked the caravan throughout one long night. Burton was fascinated less by wild beasts than by the hills of the white ant, or African termite. Rising like ruined cities out of the stony plains, these termite hills measured as high as 12 feet (3.7 meters) tall.

Ostrich in Mesai Mara, Kenya

The Somali in this part of Africa were mostly nomads who lived in temporary villages called *kraal*s. One kraal that Burton passed consisted of some 150 Somali families, 200 cows, 7,000 camels, and 11,000 sheet and goats. Curious, Burton stopped the caravan to watch this kraal pack up and migrate to better pasturelands.

Termite mound in Gambia, West Africa

69

On December 10, after nearly two weeks of traveling, Burton became ill. Bad food, bad water, and temperatures ranging from 107 degrees (42 degrees Celsius) at noon to 51 degrees (11 degrees Celsius) in the morning, had all seriously affected his health. Local remedies were tried—including burning his stomach with lit sticks—to no avail. For the rest of the journey, he would be troubled with recurring bouts of dysentery, or "colic," as he called it.

Christmas came and went. On December 27, Burton reached the village of Wilensi, home of the *jirad*, or chief, of this area. Here the caravan broke up. The women and most of the baggage would remain in Wilensi. Taking only what could be carried in one mule's saddlebags, Burton and four guides set out on December 29 for the last leg of their trip.

They stopped again in the village of Sagharrah. Burton had hoped Sagharrah's chief would lead them into Harar himself, but the man refused. Politely but firmly, he informed Burton that he "would walk into a crocodile's mouth as willingly as within the walls of Harar."

This disappointment was soon followed by another. On the morning after their arrival in Sagharrah, Burton awoke too ill to rise out of bed. Everyone was sympathetic. The chief offered millet beer—which Burton detested. His wife and daughters sacrificed a sheep, while his two sons insisted on burning Burton's stomach. A great crowd gathered to see the stranger, weeping for the evil fate that had brought him so far from his homeland to die under a tree.

For a while, Burton himself thought he might die. "Nothing indeed would have been easier . . . all required was the turning face to the wall, for four or five days.

But to expire of an ignoble colic! The thing was not to be thought of. . . ." So saying, Burton forced himself out of bed, dressed in his Arab best, and proceeded to Harar.

Before he went, however, Burton made one last decision. Wherever he had gone in Somaliland, natives had commented on his white face. It seemed he was being mistaken for a Turk—and Turks were even more hated in Africa than Englishmen. Throwing caution to the winds, Burton decided to enter Harar in his true colors as an British officer.

First he left one genuine letter in Sagharrah for Lieutenant Herne in case of emergency. Next, Burton hastily forged another letter, which he would present to the chief, or amir, of Harar. This letter, supposedly from the British agent in Aden, was to prove Burton's identity as an Englishman.

With his usual careful attention to detail, Burton noted the exact time that he came in sight of his long-awaited goal. At 2:00 P.M. on January 3, 1855, he and his four companions stopped to rest under a spreading tree. Just two miles (three kilometers) away on the crest of a hill, they could see Harar.

It was not a remarkable sight. "The spectacle . . . was a disappointment; nothing conspicuous appeared but two grey minarets of rude shape . . . but of all that have attempted, none ever succeeded in entering that pile of stones; the thorough-bred traveller . . . will understand my exultation."

Burton and his companions hurried to the city's gate. After a half hour's wait, they were admitted by the amir's porter and led to a building that, from the sound of clanking chains inside, appeared to be a prison.

View of Harar, Ethiopia

Burton's carbine pistol

There Burton waited again, while the porter disappeared within the rough stone walls. Finally the door swung open. Inside was the man sworn to put to death any foreigner entering his city—the dreaded amir of Harar!

It was no time to be timid. Burton strode boldly into a vast hall between two long rows of the amir's guards. Standing like statues, the warriors fixed Burton with fierce eyes and tightened their grips on their huge spears. Burton deliberately slowed his pace to a cool swagger, returning each stare with a fixed glare of his own. Unknown to the guards, Burton had a six-shooter concealed in his belt. If necessary to save his own life, he had no qualms about whipping out this gun and holding it steady against the amir's temple until the danger passed.

Photograph of Burton

But it wouldn't hurt to try politeness first. As he strode down the column of guards, Burton loudly gave the traditional Muslim greeting, "Peace be upon ye!"

For a moment the hall was silent. Then the dreaded amir graciously returned the greeting. The first trial had been passed. Carefully concealing his relief that he might not be killed, Burton took a moment to examine this legendary ruler. He wasn't much to look at. Thin and plain, with a yellowish complexion, wrinkled brow, and protruding eyes, the amir couldn't have been more than twenty-four or twenty-five.

Still, Burton knew better than to judge a man by appearances. He waited warily while the amir took up Burton's forged letter from the British agent. With an impatient gesture, the young ruler threw the paper aside and demanded to know what it meant.

This was the moment Burton had been dreading. In his most polished and persuasive Arabic, he began to speak. He had come in peace, he explained, not in war. He wanted neither to buy nor to sell goods. He was here simply to pay his respects to the amir—whom may Allah preserve!—and to forge a lasting friendship between the amir's people and his own.

Apparently his words satisfied the amir. With another gracious smile, Burton was excused from the royal presence. The second trial was over. Greatly relieved, Burton allowed himself to be shown to another part of the palace. This, apparently, was to be his home for as long as he was in Harar.

This palace of Yasu the Great, built in 1700 in the city of Gonder, is one of Ethiopia's many historic palaces and fortresses.

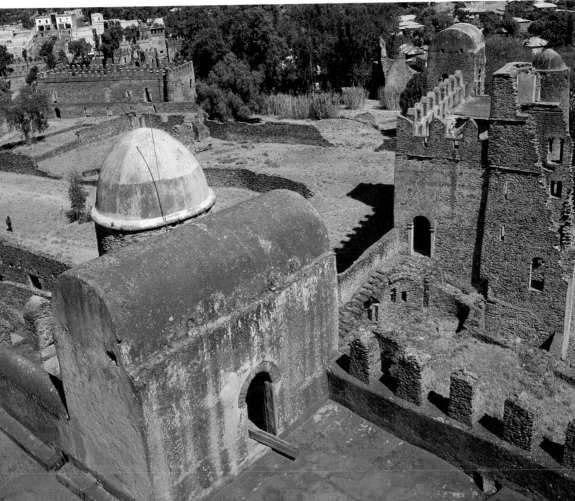

Market in the walled city of Harar, Ethiopia

That was the next big question. How long *was* he to remain in the walled city? True, the amir had not ordered him to be killed at first sight. That was encouraging—but Burton's plan called for safely getting out of, as well as into, Harar.

He brought this up at his next audience with the amir. Brushing aside the question, the amir simply said that Burton would be given a reply. And with that unsatisfactory answer, the interview ended.

Burton waited. He passed his days talking to curious citizens, repeating his Muslim prayers, and learning all he could about the town and its people. Unable to take notes, he nonetheless began learning the Harari language, a tongue spoken only by the eight thousand or so people living in the town.

All the time, Burton was aware that any misstep could be fatal. "I was under the roof of a bigoted prince whose least word was death; amongst people who detest foreigners; the only European that had ever passed over their inhospitable threshold."

Finally, after ten anxious days, he was summoned before the amir and given permission to leave. As he passed for the last time through the city's gates, Burton felt almost faint from relief. "A weight of care and anxiety fell from me like a cloak of lead," he wrote.

Impatient to reach Berbera, Burton decided to take a different route on the return trip. This included a grueling, five-day march across a harsh desert. As Burton jogged along, the sun blistering his head and his eyes closed against the fiery wind, he suffered an overwhelming longing for water. Cool, blue, bubbling water—in vain did he try to think of anything else.

A hidden water hole in the desert

Thirty-six hours went by with nothing to drink. The travelers were resigning themselves to death when Burton spotted a *katta*, or sand grouse. Knowing that these birds must drink at least once a day, he urged his men on. Stumbling with excitement, they followed eagerly after the bird.

Sure enough, the creature was headed to a hidden spring. Falling to their knees, men and mules alike drank deeply of the life-saving water. As a grateful Burton later wrote, "I have never since shot a katta."

That was the worst of the journey. A few more days' march brought them safely to the Red Sea. At 2:00 A.M. on Friday, February 9, 1855, Richard Burton was finally reunited with Herne and Stroyan in Berbera. Exhausted, he collapsed in sleep, "conscious of having performed a feat which will live in local annals for many and many a year."

Sinai Desert and the Red Sea

Chapter 7
Disappointments

Burton quickly shook off the exhaustion of his trip to Harar. As always after an expedition, he first wrote up his journal notes into a book, this one entitled *First Footsteps in Africa*. That done, he lost no time planning his next adventure.

Burton, Herne, Stroyan, and Speke spent February and March of 1855 in Aden comparing notes and making preparations. Herne and Stroyan had been successful in their Berbera missions. Speke hadn't been so lucky. Unable to speak any of the local dialects, he was forced to turn back without finding the Wadi Nogal when his native guide proved unreliable.

Still, the four men were anxious to begin the next step of their expedition. This was to be a far more ambitious project. For now, they were after no less than the source of the great Nile River!

The Nile, father of African rivers, is the longest river in the world. Rising south of the equator, it flows north through Africa for over 4,000 miles (6,437 kilometers) before emptying into the Mediterranean Sea. By 1855, people had lived along the banks of the Nile for over five thousand years.

Yet, during all that time, no one had ever known where the Nile began. Ancient Greek poets told that Phaethon, son of the sun god Helios, had driven his fiery chariot so close to the mountains of Africa that he had sent the Nile scurrying into a secret hiding place.

There were other myths, too. One Arab story put the source of the Nile high in crystal mountains, where the burning rays of the sun hid it from curious travelers. Another Arab story said the Nile flowed through eighty-five copper statues built by a king of Egypt to decorate his palace. An even older legend had it that the Nile sprang from two great lakes deep in the heart of Africa. A different legend claimed that the Nile flowed out of two great, hidden fountains.

Since ancient times, there had been written records of expeditions to find the source of the Nile. In 460 B.C., the Greek historian Herodotus sailed up the river from Egypt. Turned back by crashing waterfalls, he was unable to follow the river to its source. Other expeditions sent by such leaders as the Emperor Nero, Alexander the Great, and Julius Caesar also ended in failure. The vicious heat, huge waterfalls, endless swamps of papyrus reeds, deadly malarial fever, and hostile native peoples all took an enormous toll.

Then, in the first century A.D., a Greek merchant named Diogenes claimed that *he* had found the source of the Nile. According to his story, Diogenes reached

The ancient Greek historian Herodotus, known as the Father of History

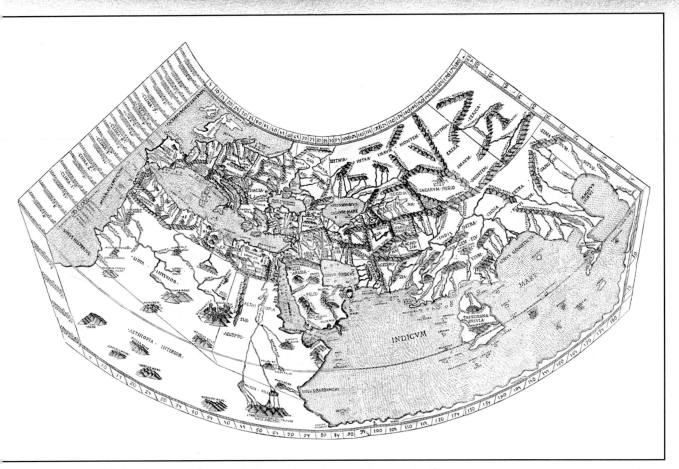

Ptolemy's map of the world. The Mountains of the Moon, giving rise to the Nile, are shown at the bottom, left of center.

Africa by accident while trying to sail home to Greece from India. Landing near the ancient trading center of Rhapta (probably near the island of Zanzibar), Diogenes began exploring. He "traveled inland for a 25-days' journey and arrived in the vicinity of two great lakes, and the snowy range of mountains whence the Nile draws its twin sources."

After Diogenes's voyage, the Syrian geographer Marinus of Tyre recorded his story. Later, the Egyptian geographer Ptolemy used this same story to make his famous world map. Ptolemy's map shows the Nile running between the Mediterranean and the equator. The great river's sources are shown as two round lakes supplied by the eternal snows atop a nearby mountain range, the Mountains of the Moon.

Claudius Ptolemaeus, known as Ptolemy—astronomer, geographer, and mathematician

81

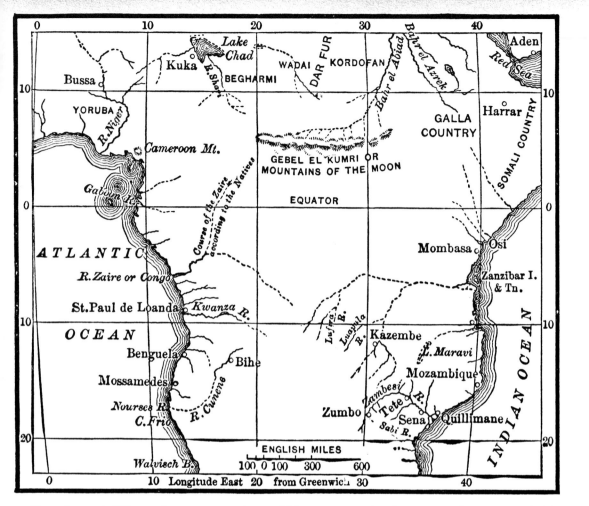

Map of central Africa as it was
known in 1840, showing the fabled
Mountains of the Moon

A twelfth-century Arab mapmaker named Al-Idrisi drew a similar map. On his map, Al-Idrisi even went so far as to include a written description of the Central African lakes.

Despite the myths, legends, and historical references, in 1855 no Westerner knew exactly where these legendary lakes were—or even if they really existed. Other, more recent European explorers had attempted to find the Nile's source, but no one had succeeded. It remained one of the great mysteries of the nineteenth century. British explorer Harry Johnson called it "the greatest geographical secret after the discovery of America."

The papyrus jungles of the Nile

This is where Richard Burton entered the picture. Like so many other explorers of his age, he had long been fascinated by the mysteries of the Nile. To his mind, traveling up the Nile from Egypt was not the way to discover the great river's sources. To his mind, it would be far better to pick a spot on the east coast near the equator and travel due west. He had even heard of just such a route while a "guest" in Harar.

Now Burton intended to put his plan into action. Setting out from Berbera, the Somali Expedition would march through Somaliland, go past Harar, and continue onward into the heart of Africa until the mystery of the Nile was solved once and for all.

Such was the goal of the four British officers as they laid their plans in the Arabian port of Aden early in 1855. By April 7, Burton, Herne, Stroyan, and Speke were safely gathered in Berbera on the East African coast. As the sun set on April 19, the expedition—by then consisting of forty men, fifty-six camels, and sundry mules and horses—was settling down for what appeared to be a quiet evening.

It was not to be. Hostile native forces attacked the camp sometime between two and three in the morning. In the ambush that followed, William Stroyan was killed and Burton, Herne, and Speke barely escaped with their lives. The Somali Expedition had ended before it even began.

Hurt and discouraged, Burton once again returned to England. After his adventures in Medina, Mecca, and Harar, he was a hero in spite of the Berbera disaster. Burton was by now one of Britain's most famous explorers. His six books were widely read, and he had been invited to speak before the Royal Geographical Society, a great honor in those days.

At this time, Great Britain was preoccupied with one of the most horrible and tragic wars of the century. The Crimean War, fought mainly in Russian Crimea on the north shore of the Black Sea, lasted from October 1853 until February 1856. This war pitted Russia against the combined forces of Britain, France, and the Turkish Ottoman Empire. The armies of both sides were commanded poorly, and over 500,000 soldiers lost their lives in the conflict.

Still, to young British officers in 1855, the war seemed a glorious opportunity to win fame and honor. So, as soon as Richard Burton's shattered jaw had mended, he set off for the Crimea. Unfortunately,

Fitzroy James Henry Somerset (Lord Raglan), commander of British troops in the Crimean War, lost the use of his sword arm in the Battle of Waterloo (1815). The raglan overcoat and raglan sleeves were named after him.

Lord Raglan, the British commander-in-chief in the Crimea, didn't think very highly of officers from the East India Company. True, the Indian army officers were the only British soldiers with much actual battle experience. But to Lord Raglan, experience didn't matter as much as noble blood. Very few of the "Indian officers," as he scornfully called them, were earls or lords or dukes. In his mind, therefore, they weren't really fit to defend Queen Victoria's realm.

So once again, Richard Burton was disappointed in his dreams of winning wartime glory. Though he eventually found a spot training Turkish soldiers, he never fought any battles himself. By April 1856, he was back in London.

Life was not a complete disappointment for Richard Burton during this time, however. Back in London, he managed to turn his Crimean experience into a book. Then, walking in the Botanical Gardens one day, he met a young lady named Isabel Arundell.

Actually, Richard and Isabel had met years before, in Boulogne, France. Richard had barely noticed Isabel, who was then just a schoolgirl. But Isabel had taken one look at the dashing Captain Burton and turned to her sister. "That man will marry me," she whispered.

For the next four years, Isabel read everything the newspapers had to say about Captain Burton's exploits. She rejoiced in his triumphs in Mecca and Medina. She feared for his safety in Harar. Hearing he was going to the Crimea, she tried, unsuccessfully, to go along too, as one of Florence Nightingale's nurses.

Isabel Arundell, later Mrs. Burton, at age seventeen

Now she was actually meeting the man of her dreams in person once again. This time, Richard Burton seemed as struck by Isabel as she was by him. In three weeks their friendship had deepened into love. For the first time in his life, Richard Burton began to talk of marriage.

Unfortunately, perhaps, for Isabel, marriage was not the only thing on Richard's mind. Even as he was courting her, he was courting the Royal Geographical Society and the East India Company for funds for yet another expedition. Richard Burton had unfinished business to take care of in Africa. The mysteries of the Nile still called to him. Before he could marry Isabel, he must put these mysteries to rest, once and for all. Late in October 1856, Richard Burton set sail for Africa once again.

Photograph of Burton holding a spear in his tent in Africa

Chapter 8
A Distant Journey
into Unknown Lands

Richard Burton's journal entry for December 2, 1856, is exuberant: "Of the gladdest moments in human life, methinks, is the departure upon a distant journey into unknown lands. Shaking off with one mighty effort the fetters of Habit, the leaden weight of Routine, the cloak of many Cares and the slavery of Home, man feels once more happy. . . . Afresh dawns the morn of life. . . ."

Burton had every reason to feel pleased. He was on his way to Zanzibar to begin a new expedition in search of the Nile. At his side was John Hanning Speke. Speke had long since recovered from the physical wounds he had received in Berbera. Privately, though, he bore other, hidden wounds to his pride and spirit. This was a secret Burton wouldn't discover for another twelve months. For the time being, he only knew that Speke was as anxious as he was to continue their adventure into deepest Africa.

It was a land as strange and remote then as outer space is today. Even the Arab slave and ivory traders, who had followed well-traveled caravan routes into Africa's interior for centuries, had never gone as far as these two intended to travel. Led on by Arab hearsay and native guides, Burton and Speke would be the first Europeans to venture into the unmapped, unknown void that was Central Africa.

Burton and Speke landed in Zanzibar on December 20, 1856. The British agent there, Lieutenant Colonel Atkins Hamerton, warned them of the dangers of their trip. Drought, famine, and disease would combine with plundering natives and torturous routes to make this expedition unlike anything either man had ever before experienced.

The warning went unheeded. "People here tell frightful stories about the dangers and difficulty of the journey," Burton wrote to the Royal Geographical Society in London. "I don't believe a word of it."

Still, he laid his plans carefully. Always before, Burton had traveled alone, or at most with a handful of native guides and porters. But a caravan into the interior of Africa was a much more complicated affair. Burton knew he should count on being away for at least a year, and possibly much longer. All the supplies he and Speke needed would have to be carried on their porters' heads or on sturdy pack animals.

The list of supplies seemed endless. They would need food, though mainly they planned to live off the land, either by hunting or by bartering with villagers. They would need weapons and ammunition—two years' worth, just to be safe. Mapping, surveying, and other scientific equipment, books and writing materials, clothing, bedding, and camp furniture were also

Animal bones bleaching in the drought-stricken Sahara Desert in Niger, west-central Africa

Captain Burton with a beard

necessary. They had carpenter's and blacksmith's tools, fishing line, two thousand fishhooks, and a small medicine chest. Finally, they carried a large cargo of cloth, brass wires, and beads to pay the porters and barter with villagers.

Burton and Speke spent six months collecting their supplies and making short exploratory trips up and down the coast. Along the way, they both managed to contract malaria. Burton also managed to master Swahili, the main language of East Africa, and to collect enough notes on Zanzibar to fill two fat volumes. As usual, nothing escaped Richard Burton's keen eye. Geography, climate, plant and animal life, politics and government, tribal life and customs—all were included in *Zanzibar: City, Island, and Coast.*

There, too, was a lengthy discussion of the slave trade that had been the cornerstone of Zanzibar's economy for centuries. Burton estimated that some twenty to forty thousand slaves passed through the island every year. One-third of them died. Another third stayed in Zanzibar. And one-third of them were exported to such places as Arabia, Egypt, Turkey, and Persia. Though the United States outlawed the West African slave trade on the Atlantic Ocean, slave trading on East Africa's Indian Ocean continued almost into the twentieth century. It was largely due to explorers like Richard Burton that the horrors of the slave trade became known to the Western world.

By June 16, 1857, Burton and Speke were ready to leave Zanzibar. Crossing the 29-mile (32-kilometer) channel to the mainland, they landed at the lovely coastal town of Bagamoyo. Two weeks later, they were

The Zanzibar slave market

Beach at Bagamoyo, Tanzania, the former slave-trade center

on their way, leading a caravan that would include 132 men, 30 mules, several camels, and a large herd of goats and cattle.

The first leg of their journey followed the familiar Arab caravan route. This well-established trail led from the Indian Ocean to the town of Kazeh (now Tabora, Tanzania), some 500 miles (805 kilometers) inland. Going from water hole to water hole, the paths were easy to follow, though progress was slow.

A typical day's march began at four o'clock in the morning with the first crowing of the cock. While Burton and Speke ate a hasty breakfast, the Arab guard turned their faces east for traditional Muslim prayers. By 5:00 A.M., the whole caravan was awake. The goats and cattle were herded together, and porters argued over who carried the heaviest load.

When everyone was ready, the drummer sounded the warning, and the head guide began the march. Next followed the heavily laden porters and the animals, while the armed guards spread out along the line. Straggling along behind came the guards' women and slaves. At the very rear rode Burton and Speke on camelback or donkey.

A day's march lasted from three to eight hours and covered two to ten miles (three to sixteen kilometers). By 11:00 A.M., the midday sun was usually too hot for further travel. The whole caravan would groan to a halt. Tents were erected for Burton and Speke, while the guards and porters put together makeshift huts. The afternoons were spent in resting, bartering with

Arab caravan stops at an oasis to rest and get water.

villagers for supplies, and writing up notes. Dinner was served in mid-afternoon, and by 8:00 P.M., the caravan had settled to sleep.

That was a typical day—if there was such a thing. Barely two weeks after they set out, both Speke and Burton came down with malaria symptoms again. Wearily, Burton wrote in his journal: "I arose weak and depressed, with aching head, burning eyes, and throbbing extremities. The new life, the alternations of damp heat and wet cold, the useless fatigue of walking, the sorry labor of waiting and reloading the asses, the exposure to sun and dew, and last, but not least . . . the wear and tear of mind at the prospect of failure, all were beginning to tell heavily upon me."

Burton and his companions on the march to find the source of the Nile, from a sketch by Burton

Termites of Tanzania

There were other troubles, too. Unseasonable rains frequently flooded the paths. Temperatures ranged from 90 degrees (32 degrees Celsius) at midday to 40 degrees (4 degrees Celsius) at night, "a killing temperature in these latitudes for half-naked and homeless men." Village chiefs demanded enormous sums before they would allow the caravan to pass through their territories. Porters deserted daily, often taking with them valuable supplies. More supplies were lost during dangerous river crossings.

Worst of all, perhaps, were the insects. Man and beast alike were "rendered wild" by the fierce bites of red and black ants. Termites destroyed their clothes, their bedding, and their tents. Mosquitoes were a daily torment, and the deadly tsetse fly a constant fear.

Besides all this, smallpox was sweeping the land, as well as mass starvation following of a long drought. Everywhere they went, Burton and Speke saw signs of the horrible devastation of these two plagues.

But these natural plagues were nothing compared to the manmade disaster of the slave trade. The misery of a slave-plundered village never failed to move Burton. "There was no vestige of building upon the spot—no sight nor sound of man—the infernal slave-trade had made a howling desert of the land," reports one journal entry. Another is even more melancholy: "A pitiable scene here presented itself. The huts were torn and half-burnt, and the ground was strewed with nets and drums, pestles and mortars, cots and fragments of rude furniture; and though no traces of blood were observed, it was evident that a commando had lately taken place there. . . . Here again the demon of slavery will reign over a solitude of his own creation."

Then the donkeys began dying. Six were lost altogether, to bee stings, hyenas, poison grasses, and exhaustion. The already over-burdened porters, many of them near starvation, refused to shoulder any extra loads. Burton and Speke were too ill to insist. "The fact is," states Burton's journal, "we were physically and morally incapacitated for any exertion beyond balancing ourselves upon the donkeys."

On November 7, 1857, the caravan finally reached Kazeh. After the poor, slave-plundered African villages they had seen for the past five months, this Arab trading center was a welcome relief. Burton, especially, was delighted. True, the Arabs of Kazeh were slavers, but they were educated, civilized men. They spoke a language Burton understood and followed a religion he admired.

Typical street in a Tanzanian town

The caravan stayed at Kazeh for five weeks. Burton was sick the whole time with "distressing weakness, hepatic derangements, burning pain, and tingling soles, aching eyes, and alternate thrills of heat and cold, [which] lasted . . . a whole month." Still, he managed to question the Arabs about which direction he should take next.

On December 14, the caravan headed west toward a lake known as the Sea of Ujiji, said to be some 200 miles (322 kilometers) away. His talks with the Arabs had convinced Burton that this great lake was indeed the source of the Nile.

After a month of difficult travel, Burton was struck with a paralyzing illness. As he shivered with racking chills, his feet and legs began to burn and swell. He

An artist's rendition of Burton's march into central Africa

felt the pinpricks of countless needles in his feet—and nothing else. Even his rib cage felt paralyzed. Eventually his hands and feet were completely numb, and his leg muscles were twisted with horrible cramps.

Barely a week later, Speke suffered "an almost total blindness, rendering almost every object enclouded as by a misty veil."

Through rain and wind, across rough, rocky terrain and roaring rivers, the two explorers pushed on. Finally, as he came to a halt at the top of a steep, thorn-covered hill, Burton saw something shining below them. Squinting, he turned to his guide and asked, "What is that streak of light that lies below?"

Solemnly, the guide replied, "I am of the opinion, that that is *the* water."

Nineteenth-century view of Ujiji on the banks of the Sea of Ujiji, now Lake Tanganyika

Lake Tanganyika

And so it was. "The whole scene suddenly burst upon my view, filling me with admiration, wonder, and delight," wrote Burton. "Forgetting toils, dangers, and the doubtfulness of return, I felt willing to endure double what I had endured."

Blind, crippled, and ill, Burton and Speke had reached the western shore of the Sea of Ujiji, Lake Tanganyika. Now all that remained was to prove that this lake truly was the source of the great Nile River.

To do this, the two explorers would need a boat. Local legend held that a large river did in fact drain out of the north end of the lake. After two months of haggling, the two men set out in two large canoes to discover this river for themselves.

It was a disappointing trip. The crew refused to take Burton and Speke the whole length of the lake,

claiming that hostile tribes to the north would surely kill them. Villagers assured the travelers that the river to the north flowed into the lake, not out of it.

Burton in a dugout on Lake Tanganyika, based on one of his drawings

Disappointed, Burton and Speke returned to Kazeh. They had found Lake Tanganyika, but they still didn't know whether or not it was the source of the Nile. They hadn't measured its length, width, or depth. They hadn't even succeeded in traveling clear around the lake. All they really knew was that the lake existed.

It wasn't enough. While Burton rested in Kazeh, he feverishly made plans for a future expedition. As things now stood, the caravan barely had enough supplies to return to Zanzibar safely. The best plan seemed to be to return to civilization, regain their health and strength, and come back later to explore the lake more thoroughly.

When Burton laid out his plan to Speke, the younger man disagreed. He had heard rumors of another large lake to the north. Burton could plan a future expedition if he wanted to. But Speke intended to visit this lake now.

If Burton was surprised at Speke's insistence, he didn't show it. Lately, he and Speke had been getting on each other's nerves. Through twelve long months they had traveled together as brothers. They had nursed each other through sickness, helped each other through hardships. Now, perhaps, it was time for a break. Burton was more than willing to remain in Kazeh. He would rest, recover, and talk with his Arab friends. Privately, he didn't think Speke would find anything in his search for this other lake. By the time Speke returned, Burton would have the caravan ready for the return trip to Zanzibar.

This decision was to be the great mistake of Richard Burton's life. On August 3, 1858, John Hanning Speke reached the shores of a huge body of water that he promptly named Lake Victoria. Without making any attempt to explore the lake, he instantly concluded that this, and not Lake Tanganyika, was the true source of the Nile. "I no longer felt any doubt," he said later, "that the lake at my feet gave birth to that interesting river, the source of which has been the object of so many explorers."

So saying, Speke returned to Kazeh. When he announced his discovery to Burton, the older man was unimpressed. He was willing to grant that Speke had indeed found a lake. He would even admit that it might be the source—or *a* source—of the Nile. But to *know* this from one glance? To go on instinct instead of scientific proof? Burton scoffed at the idea.

John Hanning Speke with Lake Victoria in the background

On this point, the breach between the two men widened into a chasm. The return trip to Zanzibar was a nightmare. All the usual difficulties of travel were intensified by the tension between the two men. To make matters worse, Speke was delirious with fever for much of the trip.

It was during the mad ravings of this fever that Burton learned Speke's true feelings for him. Ever since their adventures in Somaliland, Speke had harbored an enormous resentment for Burton. He felt that Burton blamed him, rather than his untrustworthy porter, for failing to reach the Wadi Nogal.

Lake Victoria as seen from Entebbe, Uganda

He resented the way Burton had edited his journal of that expedition. Worse, Speke was still smarting from what he saw as an insult during the Berbera incident. He believed that Burton had criticized his courage during that dreadful attack. In fact, as Burton learned during these feverish rantings, Speke felt that Burton had slighted and overlooked him repeatedly during their years together.

Burton was astonished by the revelation. Here he was, a shrewd observer of human nature. Nothing escaped his notice about the native peoples he encountered. Yet for twelve months he had failed—or refused—to see the resentment building up in his traveling companion and intimate friend. Now it was too late. After this journey to Lake Tanganyika, Speke's resentment turned to hatred.

It was a hatred that would sour the entire expedition. Speke returned to England first and made it seem that the success of the trip belonged to him, and him alone. *He* had led the expedition, and Burton had merely followed—when his health permitted. It was Speke's Lake Victoria that was the source of the Nile, not Burton's Lake Tanganyika. Lionized by an adoring public, Speke won a hero's welcome in London. More importantly, he won the Royal Geographical Society's promise of funds for future African expeditions.

Burton, meanwhile, had stayed in Aden for two weeks after Speke left. By the time he returned to London, he found, he said, "the ground completely cut from under my feet. . . . I found that everything had been done for, or rather against me. My companion now stood forth in his true colours, an angry rival. . . ."

Throughout his life, Burton had had many rivals and enemies who were only too happy to see him fail. Now some of these old enemies were flocking to Speke's side. They accused Burton of everything from cheating his African porters, to having loose personal morals, to letting down his queen and country. It was a vicious blow for a proud man.

Together, Richard Burton and John Speke had accomplished great things. They had gone where no European had gone before, suffering great hardships in the process. Together, they had discovered the great lake regions of Central Africa. But the rift between them would never be mended in their lifetimes.

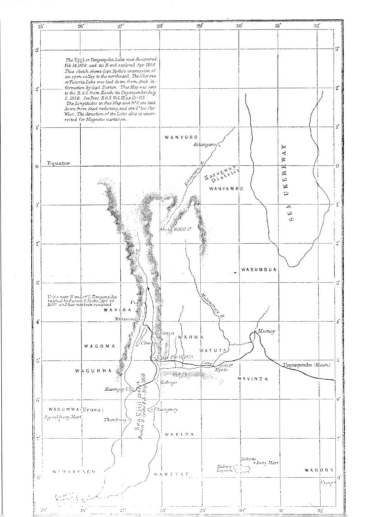

Burton's map of the area he and Speke explored in 1858, showing Ujiji sea (Lake Tanganyika) and Ukereway sea (Lake Victoria). Burton sent this map from Kazeh to the Royal Geographical Society in July 1858, before Speke had actually reached Lake Victoria.

Chapter 9
Betrayal and Beyond

Richard Burton returned to England on May 21, 1859. For nearly a year, he listened and watched as Britain toasted Speke and ignored him. Stunned by what he saw as his subordinate's betrayal, he refused to discuss the possibility that Lake Victoria might indeed be the true source of the Nile. Stubbornly, he stuck to his position that further exploration would be needed before the answer could be found.

Sadly, he watched as Speke prepared to make that further exploration. With a grant twice as large as the one Burton had received, Speke would soon be back in Africa. Britain's other great African explorer, David Livingstone, had also won a large grant. Only he, Richard Burton, was going nowhere.

It was a horrible disappointment. There were others, too. Richard's brother, Edward, had recently returned from service in the Indian army. Some terrible, unexplained accident had befallen Edward in India. Now he was home, suffering from a mysterious form of mental illness. For the remaining forty years of his life, Edward Burton would remain mute and seemingly senseless. It was a tragedy from which Richard would never truly recover.

Then there was Isabel Arundell. Richard had called on Isabel as soon as he returned from Africa. Saddened by Edward's illness and wounded by Speke's betrayal, Richard turned to Isabel for comfort. Though her love for Richard never wavered, her parents were firmly opposed to a marriage. Burton was too strange, too dangerous, too unconventional.

The combination of these disappointments was too much for Burton. As soon as he finished writing his two-volume work on the Lake Tanganyika expedition, he, too, left England. This time, he went west—to America. In an abrupt and unexpected move, Burton spent nine months traveling the United States by stagecoach. For much of this time he stayed in the Mormon capital of Salt Lake City, Utah. Exercising his usual powers of observation and analysis, Burton studied the Mormon culture and religion. As usual, he wrote a book about his experiences.

Richard Burton returned to London in December 1860. Three weeks later, he and Isabel Arundell were secretly married. For seven months, the two lived a fast-paced life, socializing with many of the great families of England.

Then, suddenly, late in August 1861, Richard left England again. This time he was off to the Spanish

Isabel Arundell Burton in 1861 at the time of her marriage

Portrait of Burton presented to him, with his wife's portrait, as a wedding gift

island of Fernando Po, off the coast of West Africa. For the next three years, Burton would serve as British consul on Fernando Po. During this time he made several short explorations into the interior of West Africa.

All in all, Burton's three years in Fernando Po resulted in nine fat volumes, including his 450-page book of African proverbs, *Wit and Wisdom in West Africa*. This was an incredible output, but the British Foreign Office wasn't impressed. Many of Burton's observations about African customs and rituals were considered shocking by proper British officials. Publicly, Burton was rebuked for being eccentric.

Privately, Burton was disappointed by his assignment to Fernando Po. This small, no-account island was so dirty, he couldn't even bring his wife there! Surely the discoverer of the Nile deserved more!

Burton still believed that he, and not John Speke, had discovered the true source of the Nile. Speke's second expedition had uncovered more evidence that Lake Victoria was, in fact, the source, but it had not proven the theory conclusively. Speke had once again failed to explore the lake thoroughly, and many of his measurements and scientific observations were faulty.

The English public was no longer as impressed with Speke as it had once been. Speke had shown himself to be a cad in his treatment of his second-in-command, James Grant. The more people learned about Speke's personality, the more they began to

John Hanning Speke (right) with James Grant in Africa

wonder if they had misjudged Richard Burton five years earlier.

The matter came to a head in September 1864. Burton was invited to debate Speke publicly about the source of the Nile. But before the debate could take place, Speke was killed in a mysterious shooting accident. The official report ruled the death an accident. Richard Burton, who had firsthand knowledge of Speke's expertise with guns, refused to believe the report. For the rest of his life, he would believe John Speke had killed himself.

Henry Morton Stanley

It was a tragic end to a senseless argument. As for the question of the Nile—it would be another twenty-two years before Henry Stanley would prove conclusively that Lake Victoria was, indeed, the true source of the Nile River. John Speke's methods may have been shoddy, but his instincts were right.

And Lake Tanganyika? It is the longest freshwater lake in the world, and the second deepest. It is also the source of the other great African river, the Congo.

Richard Burton's most celebrated explorations ended with his ill-fated trip to Lake Tanganyika. The rest of his life was spent searching for fame, glory, and honor in a different sphere.

Burton served for four years as British consul in Santos, Brazil, from 1864 to 1868. Never content with official business, he spent much of his time studying Brazilian Indian languages, translating poetry from the Portuguese—and, of course, exploring. He wandered deep into Brazil's interior, searching for gold and diamond mines. His many adventures included capsizing his canoe in a shark-infested ocean and shooting rapids no man was known to have survived during a 1,300-mile (2,092-kilometer) raft trip.

The Burtons' house in Damascus

Isabel Burton's Syrian maid

After Brazil, Burton returned to his beloved Middle East as British consul in Damascus, Syria. Though he was a popular and competent diplomat, he was dismissed from the post in controversial circumstances in 1871.

The summer of 1872 found Richard Burton in Iceland, exploring sulfur mines for a British mining speculator. In many ways, the trip was a disappointment—but, as usual, Burton came out of it with a book, this time the two-volume *Ultima Thule: or, A Summer in Iceland.*

After his return from Iceland in the fall of 1872, Burton reluctantly accepted the post of British consul

Richard Burton in his bedroom at Trieste. Here he began his translation of the Arabian Nights *in April 1884; here also he died on October 20, 1890.*

at Trieste, Italy. He was deeply humiliated by his dismissal from Damascus and viewed the Trieste assignment as punishment. Still, he and Isabel lived there happily enough for eighteen years.

During these years Burton turned to writing as a serious career. His books covered an astonishing variety of subjects—mining, engineering, archaeology, poetry, anthropology, military science, commerce, geography, mountain climbing, religion, reptiles, slavery, medicine, politics—the list seems endless. Besides writing about the places he had seen and the cultures he had studied, Burton wrote poetry and translated folk tales and legends.

Richard Burton's most famous works are those he translated from ancient Indian and Arabic sources, including his still unsurpassed version of *The Arabian Nights*. In all his writing, Burton was both scholarly and energetic, lusty and lyrical. Much of what he wrote was shocking to Victorian England. In fact, after his death, Isabel burned many of Richard's journals and unpublished manuscripts, fearing that they would damage her husband's reputation.

In 1886, Britain belatedly recognized Richard Burton for his many services. Henceforth, he would be known as Sir Richard Burton, Knight Commander of St. Michael and St. George. Four years later, on October 20, 1890, Sir Richard was dead.

Richard Burton was an unusual man in an unusual time. Linguist, scholar, author, explorer, adventurer, student of human nature—there seemed no limit to Burton's accomplishments. He filled dozens of vol-

Lady Burton in her later years

Portrait of Burton painted by Madame Gutmansthal de Benvenuti of Trieste, Italy

umes with details of his explorations and travels, published numerous translations, and wrote countless articles, pamphlets, reviews, and letters. He spoke twenty-nine languages and a dozen other dialects and was widely read in a huge variety of subjects.

Richard Burton went places no European had ever dared go before. He seemed to revel in hardship and took great pleasure in throwing himself into the language, literature, and customs of whatever people he found himself among. The fact that his stubborn, independent turn of mind kept him from winning the official recognition granted to many lesser men must have bothered him—but it didn't stop him.

As a very young man, Burton once said, "I was always of the opinion that a man proves his valor by doing what he likes." By this definition, or indeed by any other, Richard Burton was clearly a man of valor.

Appendices

Shaykh Abdullah on His Way to Arabia

Burton, as Shaykh Abdullah (left), suffered many hardships and absurd situations on his journey from Alexandria to Cairo, through the Suez Desert, and on to Medina and Mecca. He also described the sublime joys of desert travel. Here are some of his recollections:

Not without a feeling of regret, I left my little room among the white myrtle blossoms and the rosy oleander flowers with the almond scent . . . and mounted in a "trap" which looked like a cross between a wheelbarrow and a dog-cart, drawn by a kicking, jibbing, and biting mule, I set out for the steamer. . . .

At Cairo . . . I became a Pathan. I was born in India of Afghan parents, who had settled there, and I was educated at Rangoon. . . . I knew all the languages that I required to pass me, Persian, Hindostani, and Arabic. . . . I hired a couple of camels, and put my Meccan boy and baggage on one, and I took the other. I had an eighty-four mile ride in midsummer, on a bad wooden saddle, on a bad dromedary, across the Suez Desert.

In the desert . . . the mind is influenced through the body. Though your mouth glows, and your skin is parched, yet you feel no languor, the effect of humid heat; your lungs are lightened, your sight brightens, your memory recovers its tone, and your spirits become exuberant. Your fancy and imagination are powerfully aroused, and the wildness and sublimity of the scenes around you, stir up all the energies of your soul. . . . Your morale improves; you become frank and cordial, hospitable and single-minded; the hypocritical politeness and the slavery of Civilization are left behind you in the City. Your senses are quickened; they require no stimulants but air and exercise. . . .

The Nile: A Mapmaker's Mystery

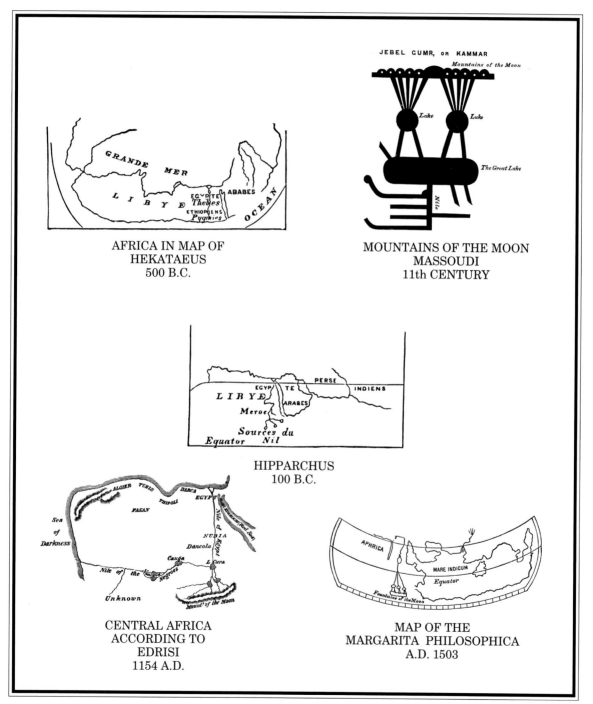

AFRICA IN MAP OF
HEKATAEUS
500 B.C.

MOUNTAINS OF THE MOON
MASSOUDI
11th CENTURY

HIPPARCHUS
100 B.C.

CENTRAL AFRICA
ACCORDING TO
EDRISI
1154 A.D.

MAP OF THE
MARGARITA PHILOSOPHICA
A.D. 1503

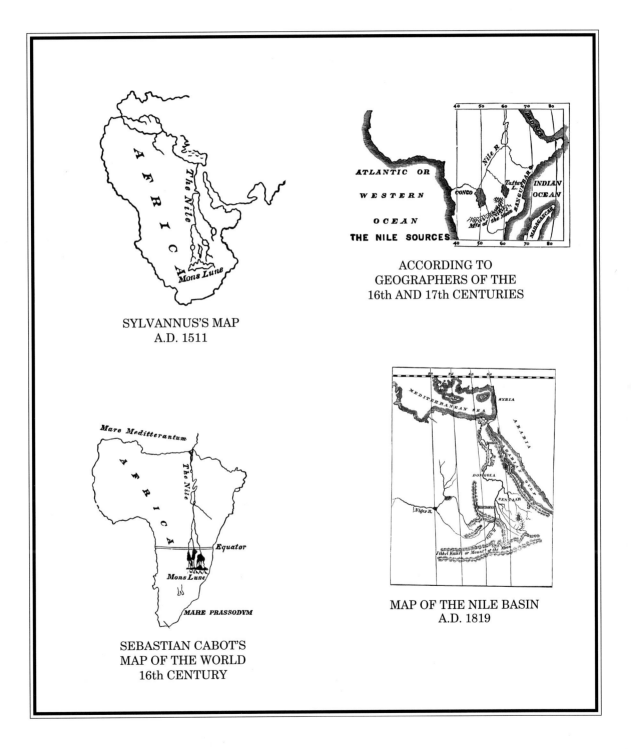

SYLVANNUS'S MAP
A.D. 1511

ACCORDING TO
GEOGRAPHERS OF THE
16th AND 17th CENTURIES

SEBASTIAN CABOT'S
MAP OF THE WORLD
16th CENTURY

MAP OF THE NILE BASIN
A.D. 1819

Timeline of Events in Burton's Lifetime

1821—Richard Francis Burton is born at Torquay, England; within a year, his family moves to France

1830—The Burton family returns to England

1838—Queen Victoria begins her long reign as queen of England

1840—Burton enters Oxford University

1842—Burton is expelled from Oxford; the Treaty of Nanking ends the Opium War between Great Britain and China; Burton joins the Indian army, going on secret missions disguised as a native

1848—Burton takes a leave from the army

1853—Disguised, Burton visits the Muslim holy cities of Mecca and Medina

1853-1856—Great Britain battles Russia in the Crimean War

1854—Burton leaves for the forbidden city of Harar, reaching it in January 1855

1855—Hoping to find the source of the Nile River, Burton, Speke, and two other officers prepare for their Somali Expedition, which ends in Berbera before it begins; Burton goes to the Crimea but does not engage in combat

1857—Burton and John Hanning Speke leave Zanzibar to find the source of the Nile

1858—Burton and Speke reach Lake Tanganyika; leaving Burton, Speke discovers Lake Victoria, declaring it to be the source of the Nile

1859—Speke returns to London a hero

1860—Burton travels to America, where he studies the Mormon culture in Utah; he returns to England and marries Isabel Arundell

1861—Burton serves as British consul on the West African island of Fernando Po

1864—John Hanning Speke mysteriously dies; Burton takes the post of British consul in Santos, Brazil

1868—Burton becomes British consul in Damascus, Syria

1872—Burton is appointed British consul in Trieste, Italy, and holds this post until his death

1886—Burton is knighted, acquiring the title Sir Richard Burton, Knight Commander of St. Michael and St. George

1890—Richard Burton dies in Trieste, Italy

Glossary of Terms

amir—Also spelled *emir*; Asian or African ruler

barter—To trade goods for goods

breach—A break or gap

cad—An impolite, ungentlemanly person

caravan—A long string of travelers, often with pack animals

chasm—A deep separation or division

cholera—A bacterial disease causing severe intestinal pain and diarrhea

delirious—Mentally disturbed, with strange speech and vision

dervish—Member of an Islamic brotherhood of mystics; a dervish who wanders from place to place and begs is known as a *faqir*

dysentery—A painful intestinal infection

epidemic—A rapidly spreading disease

intrepid—Brave, fearless, and enduring

linguist—A person who speaks several languages or who studies human speech

lionized—Treated as if very interesting and important

malaria—Disease accompanied by chills and fever and transmitted by a certain mosquito

minaret—A tall, thin tower on a Muslim mosque

monsoon—Heavy seasonal rains that fall in southern Asia and around the Indian Ocean

Muslim—A follower of the Islamic religion

rift—A break or division in a land surface or between people

saber—A sword with a curved blade

surly—In a gloomy or resentful mood

taboos—Actions forbidden for religious or superstitious reasons

Bibliography

There are no children's books about Richard Burton besides this one. However, both children and adults enjoy *The Arabian Nights*, or *The Thousand and One Arabian Nights*, of which Burton made a famous translation. The following books give some background for Burton's explorations:

Goldston, Robert. *The Sword of the Prophet: History of the Arab World from Mohammed to the Present*. NY: Dial Press, 1979.

Langley, Andrew. *Explorers of the Nile*. Morristown, NJ: Silver Burdett, 1982.

Murphy, E. Jefferson. *Understanding Africa*. NY: Crowell, 1978.

Older students may be interested in reading Burton's own writings or reading about him in one of the following adult books:

Brodie, Fawn. *The Devil Drives: A Life of Sir Richard Burton*. NY: Norton, 1967.

Burton, Isabel. *The Life of Captain Sir Richard Burton*. 2 volumes. Reprint of 1898 edition. Wakefield, NH: Longwood, 1977.

Rice, Edward. *Captain Sir Richard Francis Burton: The Secret Agent Who Made the Pilgrimage to Mecca, Discovered the Kama Sutra and Brought the Arabian Nights to the West*. NY: Scribner, 1990.

Note: The 1989 film *Mountains of the Moon* tells the story of Burton's African expedition with John Hanning Speke.

Index

Page numbers in boldface type indicate illustrations.

Picture Identifications for Chapter Opening Spreads

6-7—Lake scenery in central Africa

20-21—Tours, France, where Burton spent his early childhood

30-31—Great Britain's Oxford University

36-37—A bazaar in Delhi, India

50-51—Desert caravan in Rajasthan, India

60-61—Lake Abbiata in the Rift Valley of Ethiopia

78-79—Murchison Falls on the Nile River, Uganda

88-89—The Zambezi River just above Victoria Falls

106-107—Victoria Falls on the Zambezi River, Zimbabwe

Picture Acknowledgments

The Bettmann Archive—2, 18, 19, 45, 65, 73

© Cameramann International, Ltd.—88-89

Historical Pictures Service, Chicago—5, 6-7, 33, 36-37, 38 (top), 39, 40, 63, 64, 85, 91, 99, 110, 111, 116

North Wind Picture Archives—4, 12, 13, 15, 20-21, 25, 26, 27, 29, 32, 35, 38 (bottom), 41, 42, 44, 46, 47, 49, 53, 54, 57, 58, 59, 67, 72 (margin), 76, 80, 81 (2 pictures), 82, 83, 86, 87, 92, 94, 95, 98, 100, 101, 103, 105, 109 (2 pictures), 112 (2 pictures), 113, 114, 115, 118-119 (9 pictures)

Odyssey Productions: © Robert Frerck—50-51

Photri—9, 28, 60-61, 68 (margin), 69 (bottom), 72 (top), 75, 93, 97, 106-107

H. Armstrong Roberts—30-31, 74

SuperStock—43, 66, 78-79, 90, 104

Valan Photos: © Stephen J. Krasemann—68 (top), 69 (margin), 96; © Richard Nowitz—77

About the Author

Charnan Simon grew up in Ohio, Georgia, Oregon, and Washington State. She holds a B.A. degree in English Literature from Carleton College in Northfield, Minnesota, and an M.A. in English Literature from the University of Chicago. She worked for children's trade book companies after college and became the managing editor of *Cricket* magazine before beginning her career as a free-lance writer. Ms. Simon has written dozens of books and articles for young people and especially likes writing—and reading—history, biography, and fiction of all sorts. She lives in Chicago with her husband and two daughters.